BRITISH RAILWAYS

PAST AND PRESENT

The
North East

D1103382

by Peter J Robinson & Ken Groundwater

Silver Link Publishing Ltd

FAWCETT STREET JUNCTION, SUNDERLAND: Top: LNER 'B1' 4—6—0 No. 61014 *Oribi* **climbs the 1 in 78 curve (dating from 1879) from Sunderland Central station, to join the 1852 Penshaw — Hendon route. The Sunderland — Penshaw passenger service survived until May 1964 and the two tracks on the left were subsequently severed during rationalisation in 1965, leaving the single track (on the right) to the dock, which** carried coal traffic until closure in 1984. This junction was the site of Fawcett Street station, which pre-dated Sunderland Central by 27 years, and which was located on the embankment running through the centre bridge arch. The two chimneys seen above the bridge parapet in the 'past' picture were part of the station building. The latter day view (above) shows the abandoned junction site on May 29 1986. *Ian S. Carr/D. Black.*

CONTENTS

FRONT COVER: ANNFIELD PLAIN: If any picture could be said to summarise the closing years of north-eastern steam in action, then this would be a very strong candidate: a pair of Britain's most powerful locomotives are working hard to move 500 tons of iron ore up a 1 in 35 gradient past Annfield East Junction, over a section of railway originally designed for rope haulage in 1834. In May 1965, Riddles Class 9F 2—10—0s Nos. 92065, assisted in the rear by sister engine No. 92062, are raising the echoes amid the rich mineral country of West Durham, where Stephenson's creation enjoyed its early commercial success. We have allowed ourselves the indulgence of using more Tyne-Dock — Consett photos elsewhere in these pages, for this was a route of exceptional historical importance, where exceptional locomotives and railwaymen did much sterling work. We returned to this location on March 20 1987, to find the sad sight shown in the inset view. A few lengths of fencing and the stub of the signalpost remains, but otherwise nothing of the railway hardware survives. At the time of going to press, Durham planners were considering making the trackbed into a countryside trail. *Both: PJR.*

TITLE PAGE: The taxing 1 in 40 gradient of Seaton Bank, between Ryhope and the large NCB complex at South Hetton, was one of the last locations in the North East where 'pyrotechnics' were guaranteed by steam engines working empty coal wagons to the pithead. In this picture, the last surviving 'Q6' 0—8—0, No. 63395, is seen attacking the bank during the last weeks of steam operation, with a particularly varied rake of wagons. In complete contrast, the modern picture of Class 56 No. 56118, climbing the bank with MGR 'empties', seems very clinical, with a uniform train and no visibly apparent effort by the locomotive. However, when No. 56118's wagons are filled, its payload will be more than three times the amount formerly handled by steam traction. The track has been singled, and the telegraph poles removed in the intervening years. No. 63395 survives today in the care of the North Eastern Locomotive Preservation Group, based on the North Yorkshire Moors Railway. *Both: PJR.*

British Library Cataloguing in Publication Data

British railways past and present.

Vol. 4: The North East
1. Railroads – Great Britain – History
I. Groundwater, Ken   II. Robinson, Peter
385'.0941 HE3018

ISBN 0-947971-17-3

First published in the United Kingdom, November 1987
Reprinted November 1988
Reprinted May 1991
Reprinted January 1993

Printed and bound in Great Britain

INTRODUCTION

THE world today changes rapidly and this is particularly true here in the North-East of England, an area once synonymous with railways, mining and heavy industry. Traditionally, even those of us who live in the region are sometimes prone to view ourselves in a rather grey light, as being surrounded by skulking shipyard cranes, smouldering pit ash-heaps and regimental rows of 'hooses', all ultimately leading the mind's eye to the wide, ancient and normally deserted windswept beaches, where the sky and sea meet somewhere beyond the Vane Tempest winding house. We do ourselves little justice!

In the 1960s, we were the final few to witness and record the dying rays of the industrial sunset over some of the north east's scenes of rough beauty. There were many casualties, some of which were spectacular, such as the loss of the Consett Iron Company, served in later steam days by the thunderous power of Robert Riddles' mighty Class 9F 2—10—0s, as shown on the cover of this book. The red dust at Consett settled for the last time in 1984 and today the enormous works has been completely erased from the landscape. Once so immense and permanent, those who witnessed the operations at Consett and then visit the site today find it difficult to believe that such substantial industrial muscle could be so utterly eradicated. More than 150 years of hard work has simply been swept away, and already, a generation is growing to whom Consett's Works exists only in the memories of their parents and in the pages of books like this. Consett in many ways epitomised the heavy industry on which the north east of England built its skills and reputation, and its demise throws much of the region's experience over the last two decades into very sharp focus indeed.

Through the medium of 'past and present' pictures, featuring the same location, photographed many years apart, this book reviews the changing face of the north east over the last 30 years or so. Some railways are still at work, although almost invariably they have been pruned, stripped of much lineside equipment and carry less traffic, whilst other routes have been closed and either abandoned or redeveloped for other uses, including houses, light industrial workshops, even footpaths. The contrast in many of the cases is very striking indeed, and will probably cause surprise even for people who know these areas well.

The changes and cutbacks on the railways and in industry generally have left much of the north east searching for new direction as traditional activities and businesses have declined, with the result that unemployment in the late 1980s is rivalling the depressing days of the 1930s. In some areas, many small businesses are hard at work in small units, some of which occupy former railway land, as illustrated, for example, by our photographs depicting Alnwick and St. Johns Chapel.

British Rail has established its own next phase of major development, and in the 1990s hopes to be 'getting there' in Paris Gard du Nord by 1730 hours 'on the dot', via the Channel Tunnel. Whether this development, will, as promised, benefit northern industrial regions as well as the south remains to be seen.

Although the end of steam traction in 1967 in this region radically changed the appearance of the trains themselves in the north east, the subsequent rationalisation of trackwork, modernisation of major stations and rationalisation of signalling carried out subsequently has undoubtedly done much more to change the atmosphere and appearance of the railway as a whole. The removal of signals, lineside point rodding, traditionally gated level crossings and other peripheral equipment has stripped the railway of much of its character. Changes continue to affect the railway, and since the miner's strike, for example, vacuum-braked hopper wagons have been almost completely replaced by 32-tonne air-braked Merry-Go-Round Wagons, capable of running at 60mph.

However, as this book went to press it appeared that the downward curve of the business graph for the coal sector at least had 'levelled out', and, together with electrification of the East Coast Main Line, the staging of the National Garden Festival (not to mention the relatively new operations of Nissan and Komatsu) BR in the North East was looking forward to a rather rosier future.

The book *Freight Only* (published by SLP in 1987) illustrates in detail the rejuvenation of the Railfreight business, whilst in the passenger sector, although BR has lost some traffic to the Newcastle Metro system, it has won some business, such as at Heworth and Dunston. Also, on August 3 1987, a new station was opened at Gatesheaed Metro-Centre.

Whatever is in store for the North East over the next three decades, we hope that success will return, and that 'Geordies' will once again have a solid economic and industrial foundation in which can be found both the pride and the prosperity which once attached to shipbuilding, steelmaking and coalmining. In the meantime, we hope readers will enjoy our pictorial examination of social and industrial change in the north east.

PJR,   *KG,*
Tynemouth, September 1987.   *Gateshead, 1987.*

CONSETT: Consett's remote iron and steel works, although served well by its steeply-graded railways, suffered from huge costs incurred by the need to transport raw materials to its furnaces from a variety of sources of increasing distance. Top: In Summer 1964, after its difficult journey from Tyne Dock with 500 tons of Peruvian ore, assisted by a sister '9F', No. 92064 reverses slowly away from the discharge gantry to take water from the tower adjacent to the tender before using the nearby triangle to reverse for its return trip to Tyne Dock. On viewing the scene today, it is difficult to believe that such major industrial activity ever occurred here. The later picture was taken in bleak, wintry conditions on March 10 1987. *Both: PJR.*

BERWICK — MORPETH

THE ROYAL BORDER BRIDGE, adjacent to the station at Berwick upon Tweed, appears a much more obvious England/Scotland Border than the bleak point on the clifftop at Marshall Meadows where Anglo-Scottish trains actually cross the border. Above: Class V3 2—6—2T No. 67617 runs into Berwick on August 2 1957 with a stopping train from St. Boswells, which will have reversed at Tweedmouth. *A.R. Thompson.*

Above: The signal gantry has disappeared and the trees have grown considerably, but otherwise little had changed at Berwick on August 4 1987 as the 0800 Kings Cross — Aberdeen raced over the bridge at the current maximum speed of 70mph. During consultations prior to electrification, there was considerable controversy with the planning authorities about the harmful visual impact of overhead catenary on the Royal Border Bridge. Planners at one stage actually suggested, it is reported, that a 'break' should be left in the catenary on the Border Bridge, with the trains coasting across without power! Quite how southbound 'stopping' trains were to re-start from Berwick upon Tweed under such circumstances was obviously overlooked! *PJR.*

SEAHOUSES: This coastal station, south of Berwick on Tweed, was the terminus of a four-mile branch which diverged from the Anglo-Scottish main line at Chathill. Known originally as the North Sunderland Light Railway, the operating company was still independent from the LNER as late as the 1930s. Our 'past' picture shows Seahouses circa 1920, with an up train standing at the platform, in the charge of 0—6—0ST *Bamburgh*, Manning Wardle No. 1394, built in 1898. In 1934, the Company purchased an Armstrong Whitworth 95hp diesel electric locomotive (No. D25 of 1933), with the help of Lord Armstrong of Bamburgh. Bought in an attempt to improve profitability, the locomotive was subsequently named *Lady Armstrong*. In 1939, the LNER took over operations. The branch became part of the BR system in 1948, but only survived until October 27 1951, when Class Y7 0—4—0T No. 68089 worked the final day's holiday-makers to and fro for the last time. The station site today is occupied by a car park, as illustrated in the June 1987 view. *Northumberland Record Office/PJR.*

AMBLE JUNCTION: An interesting scene at Amble Junction in 1924 (below) showing the signalbox (opened 1900) with Signalman J. Humble at the window. Located 26½ miles north of Newcastle and straddling the East Coast Main Line, this box controlled the Junction for Amble, used for passenger traffic until 1930. The cabin closed three years later. Note how signal wires were carried overhead to the posts on the right and thence descended to the more conventional ground route to the signals concerned. The cabin remained intact after closure until it was destroyed by fire on August 20 1937, leaving only the main girders, which were not dismantled until October 1942, when scrap metal was needed for the war effort. The Amble (or Warkworth) branch (five miles in length) was opened for mineral traffic on September 5 1849, when the first coals from Broomhill were transported to Amble Staithes for shipment. *J.F. Mallon.*

Right: Today's scene at Amble gives no hint of Signalman Humbles' honest endeavours to keep the traffic moving, or his efforts to keep the 62 levers in the McKenzies & Holland frame in immaculate condition. On June 30 1987, snowplough-fitted Class 47 No. 47006 passes with the 6X51 Leith — St. Neots (coated pipes) service. The trackbed of the Amble branch is now a reserved road for opencast mining trucks. *PJR.*

NORTH BLYTH LOCOMOTIVE SHED: Planned in the latter years of the 19th century, this motive power depot was originally designed to house around 20 engines, but increasing traffic soon prompted a larger allocation, and many locomotives were regularly stored outside. North Blyth was always primarily a freight shed, South Blyth having taken over its three passenger duties in the 1930s. Towards the end of steam traction in the mid-1960s, North Blyth became home to around two dozen '[27' 0—6—0s, as illustrated (top) in Spring 1966. Stabled around the turntable are 'J27s' Nos. 65813, 65789, 65880 (the last surviving superheated example), 65802 and 65815, accompanied by (centre) a solitary 'K1' 2—6—0. Following steam's last day at North Blyth (September 9 1967), the roundhouse was used to house diesels until January 29 1968 when the nearby new Cambois diesel depot opened. As shown above, nothing remains today of the old steam shed. *Both: PJR.*

NEWBIGGIN ON SEA is located deep in the Northumberland coalfield, 2 miles and 44 chains east of 'Coal City' — Ashington. Newbiggin is still for many people a favourite holiday location, and in the past it often provided the only view of the sea many miners children enjoyed when times were hard. The Blyth & Tyne Railway Railway Company had originally planned to expand north from Ashington, direct to Warkworth Harbour, and obtained Parliament's blessing for this idea, but it never came to fruition. Instead, the railway was extended east through Woodhorn and Newbiggin to serve the local collieries, and the route was ready for the 'bucket and spade brigade' by March 1872. Two years later the NER absorbed the BTR and through the LNER period and into BR days, the seaside terminus worked well, if unspectacularly. A victim of the Beeching cutbacks, the station closed in November 1964. Our 1950s photograph (above) recalls the leisurely atmosphere of the branch with 'G5' 0—4—4T No. 67347 standing at the platform. *O. Metcalfe.*

Above: There is little indication today that Newbiggin on Sea station ever existed. In March 1987, only the buildings on the skyline helped to positively identify the location. *PJR.*

LINTON COLLIERY, directly north of Ashington, was linked to the coal company's internal railway of approximately 20 miles in length and was served by the NCB's private passenger service, which operated 'dirty' trains from the pithead to the baths, and clean ones at both start-of-shift and also from the baths! These trains, comprised of ancient stock hauled by an assortment of tank engine shunters, could often be seen bowling along with doors swinging open! Below: In early 1963, RSH 0—6—0T No. 31 (then only 15 years old) leaves Linton with an Ashington-bound 'clean' train. No. 31 was preserved and can now be seen on the North Yorkshire Moors Railway, named *Meteor*. *PJR*.

Left: The same location in March 1987, with only the vandalised remains of the winding house on the horizon to indicate that the colliery ever existed. The single track was used latterly by the ex-BR NCB Class 14 diesel hydraulic shunters from Ashington, but their withdrawal in December 1986 meant a sudden end to this fascinating private rail complex, much to the regret of those who remember the mixed assortment of engines and GNR or NER coaches which ran on these lines many years after disposal by their parent companies. BR still has access to Ashington colliery from the Butterwell curve, linked to the main line north of Morpeth. *PJR*.

SLEEKBURN, between Bedlington and North Seaton, was the location of the triangular Junction for the 'Great-Way-Round' to North Blyth and Cambois. In steam days 'J27' 0—6—0s and 'Q6' 0—8—0s made seemingly endless processions along the three routes, with numerous mineral trains linking the region's collieries, shipping staithes and power stations. There was a constant shortage of empty wagons and pits would be frequently vying with their neighbours to obtain 'trucks' before coal had to be 'teemed-by' (sorted on the ground), an extremely labour intensive operation. Top: On a glorious evening on May 28 1965, 'J27' 0—6—0 No. 65879 takes the main line towards Ashington at West Sleekburn, with coal from the Backworth complex. The signalbox from which the 'past' picture was taken has gone, together with the access siding into Bomarsund Colliery. In the modern scene (above) Class 56 No. 56127 leaves the adjacent power station branch, bound for Tyne Yard with empty MGR wagons for Swalwell. *Both: PJR.*

NEWSHAM: This station, the junction for Blyth, opened in 1847, with passenger links to Monkseaton, Bedlington and the New Bridge Street terminal of the Blyth & Tyne Railway, and Newbiggin on Sea. The 'past' picture (above) features stalwart branch engine No. 67323, a 'G5' 0—4—4T, which figures in many pictures of Blyth & Tyne branch services, and which survived until 1958. Below: On Wednesday May 13 1987, Class 37 No. 37030 sweeps past the cleared site of Newsham station with 'BBA' wagons conveying aluminium ingots from the Lynemouth Smelter, destined for Cardiff Tidal sidings, via Tyne and Tees yards. The little station closed on November 2 1964 and there is no sign today that it ever existed. *Dave Tyreman Collection/PJR.*

THE iron ore traffic from Tyne Dock to Consett was one of the most impressive and spectacular of the north east's extremely varied railway operations. During the 1960s especially, after Robert Riddles mighty '9F' 2—10—0s had taken over from NER 'Q7' three-cylinder 0—8—0s, many enthusiasts visited the north east to view the spectacle for themselves. In this section, we pay tribute to the engines and railwaymen of the Tyne Dock — Consett route, paying particular attention to the iron ore traffic.

TYNE DOCK — CONSETT

TYNE DOCK: The Stanhope & Tyne Railway first built coal 'drops' in the South Shields area about a mile north-east of Tyne Dock, and it became clear as the world demand for coal surged in the mid-1800s, that a much larger coal-shipping dock was needed to minimise delays and increase flows. Consequently, from 1834, development followed rapidly and a Tyne Dock Company was formed on July 1 1839 by Act of Parliament, but unfortunately this plan fell foul of the Stanhope & Tyne company's financial difficulties. Later, in 1849, we learn that "excavations for the Tyne Docks were suspended", but, a new Act, obtained in 1854, enabled the resumption of work in the summer of 1855. In January 1859, coal finally started to pass through the newly-completed Tyne Dock, actually at Jarrow Slake.

Designed by Mr. T. Harrison, who was a member of a great north-eastern railway family, the dock was soon declared to be the largest in the world and remained so until the late 19th century. It consisted of a basin of 50 acres, sufficient for up to 500 vessels, and there were four jetties. At long last, the slow single wagon 'drops' of the previous era were superseded and the stage was set for shipments of minerals through the Tyne to leap from four million tons in 1859 to 10½ million tons in the next 30 years. Thus, the River Tyne was transformed from little more than a deep stream into "The Queen of Aal Thu Rivas", as the Geordies might have described it!

Opposite page, upper: Our first illustration dates from the turn of the century, when white Scandinavian four-masted timber ships were still a common sight. The railway runs from Tyne Dock 'Bank-Top' around into the Dock Goods area, with standard NER signals prominent. Interesting details include the circular reservoir in the left foreground, used by the NER as a locomotive water supply. This reservoir, although abandoned and partly filled, can still be seen in the 1965 view. *Beamish North of England Open Air Museum.*

Opposite page, lower: Tyne Dock operations during 1965, with Riddles 2—10—0 No. 92060 working hard with nine loaded iron-ore cars, assisted in the rear by a Class 08 diesel shunter. The trains were loaded under the ore gantry, visible in the background, to the left of the dock cranes. *PJR.*

Below: A latter-day view of Tyne Dock, on June 9 1987, with Class 56 No. 56132 climbing the gradient with a train of MGR 'empties', bound for South Hetton. Note that much of the dock area beyond the train has been filled, compared with the previous view, and that the area of the former circular reservoir has also been filled, almost to rail level. Further infilling off to the left of this view resulted in the construction of the Tyne Central Coal Terminal, opened on March 11 1985. The coal drops, visible on the right of the 1965 view, have been swept away, and there have been many changes on the far dockside. *PJR.*

GREEN LANE (TYNE DOCK LOCOMOTIVE SHED): Tyne Dock shed was built primarily to provide traction for the thousands of wagons coming and going weekly from Tyne Dock, once the world's biggest coal shipping complex. Extensions were quickly needed in 1871, and then again in 1877, with the result that, as at Gateshead and Heaton, Tyne Dock shed assumed the ramshackle 'add-on' appearance which belied the internal smooth efficiency of shed routine. *Malcolm Dunnett.*

Top: Our December 1963 picture shows '9F' 2—10—0 No. 92097 fighting for grip on frosty rails with a mixed goods bound for Park Lane, Gateshead, passing under the 71-lever Green Lane Bridge Cabin. In the modern picture (above) taken in July 1987, the railway has retreated and the complex junctions and signalling have become a simple two-track layout, whilst a private housing development now occupies the shed site. The surviving track on the left is still used by trains running to the Tyne Central Coal Terminal, whilst on the right is the last remnant of the 1834 Stanhope & Tyne route, now used only as far as Boldon Colliery (Closed) coal stocking ground, and which crosses the main coastal route on the flat crossing at Pontop. *KG.*

SOUTH PELAW, just north of Chester le Street, was a fascinating railway 'crossroads', where rails running west from the coast crossed the ECML, and then divided to run inland, before joining again at Annfield Plain to approach Consett. Our atmospheric 'past' view of South Pelaw typifies the hustle and bustle of a normal weekday at this busy centre. In the left foreground, we see a 'Q6' 0—8—0 coming into the scene from the Washington Pits with 'empties' on the Stanhope & Tyne route, whilst in the background, other goods engines, near South Pelaw Colliery, await the road for Consett, via Beamish. Banking engines would stand in their siding until they were required either to assist trains of 100 tons or more in the Beamish direction, or assist 'empties' up to Stella Gill. In these days South Pelaw was constantly busy, which partly explains the eerie silence of the abandoned location today, as shown in our July 1987 picture. *Malcolm Dunnett/KG.*

PELTON: This location was a couple of miles from South Pelaw (see page 17) on the 1893 diversionary railway, requested by the local population, which connected with the original line at Annfield Plain. The gradient at Pelton averaged 1 in 60, and in this magnificent view, during November 1965, Class 9F No. 92064, and its 'Q6' 0—8—0 banking engine are working hard to maintain momentum in readiness for the approaching steeper climb through Beamish. The load of 400 tons comprises oil tanks from Jarrow's Shell Mex Depot, bound for the Consett Fell Coke works. Before the '9Fs' came, when the NER 'Q7' 0—8—0s had reigned supreme on this section, the LNER's 1924 Freight Train Loading Circular stated that 'Q7's' were authorised to haul 700 tons over these gradients, providing another 'Q7' was available as a banking engine! Today, following track removal in 1985, only the houses remain as witnesses to the railway history, as pictured on March 19 1987.

BEAMISH: The 'past' picture, taken in the early part of the 20th century, proves that this route was used for passenger services, as well as the very well-known mineral and freight services! In January 1881, local people petitioned the NER to provide a service into nearby towns such as Chester le Street and Birtley. It was suggested that: "slight deviation of the existing route to the north of Annfield Plain by way of Kyo, Shield Row, Pelton and Ouston, forming a junction with the Team Valley railway, would meet the convenience of the main portion of the population." Six years passed before the NER's resulting Bill received the royal assent and the new, very steep route (opened 1894) had stations at Pelton, Beamish, Shield Row (for the Stanley area) and Annfield. Our 'past' picture shows Beamish in 1910. *Beamish North of England Open Air Museum.*

Beamish Station. 3824

Left: The passenger service at Beamish survived until September 21 1953, and following complete closure on March 17 1984, the track was lifted, leaving nature to reclaim the formation as shown in the 1987 view. *A.R. Thompson.*

BEAMISH: This location, about 300 yards west of Beamish station, illustrates the point at which the railway burrows beneath the Beamish — Causey Road through a short tunnel, close to the remains of a local Colliery. Above: In June 1967, Riddles 'Austerity' 2—8—0 No. 90009 storms upgrade through the cutting with a short but heavy engineers train; the 'WDs' were not particularly popular with Tyne Dock crews, but served their purpose well.

Right: On May 12 1987, the thunder of a hard-working 'Austerity' seemed difficult even to imagine, when the route of the railway was photographed, returning to nature. The pithead gear on the hilltop has disappeared and the trackbed is in use as a bridleway, and as this book went to press, plans were in hand to turn the formation into a Countryside Commission Walk. *Both PJR.*

ANNFIELD EAST: A magnificent spectacle (above) as a pair of Riddles '9F' 2—10—0s (No. 92065 as the train engine No. 92062 assisting) storm through Annfield in May 1965 en route to Consett with a 500-tons ore train. This is a rear view of the train pictured on the front cover of this book. The train has just ascended a short 1 in 35 section to reach the easier 1 in 53 average climb of the original 1834 Stanhope & Tyne Railway — note the gradient post on the left. The ten '9Fs' specially-modified with air compressors (for working the discharge mechanism) used on the ore trains worked their last Consett duties on November 19 1966, No. 92063 working the last train from Tyne Dock with some ceremony (see page 5). *PJR.*

Above: This modern view at Annfield East, in May 1987, shows that weeds and small shrubs are gradually taking possession of the once neatly maintained permanent way. The roar of the '9Fs' is long gone. *PJR.*

This page, upper & lower: In February 1964, Riddles Class 9F 2—10—0 No. 92064 makes spectacular progress up the bank from Consett Low yard with a heavy train of steel, assisted at the rear by a banking engine. In the background can be seen silhouetted the chimneys and huge sheds of the enormous works, and some of the terraced houses of the workforce. To look at the vast emptiness at this location today, you would be hard-pressed to realise that this mighty complex had ever existed. Only the half-buried overbridge in the middle distance survives as a common feature between these two scenes. The mighty iron horse of Stephenson and Riddles has given way to a solitary white horse in the later view, which depicts the site on June 15 1987. No. 92064 was withdrawn in November 1966, when steam traction to Consett ended, and the 2—10—0 was scrapped by Thompson's, of Stockton on Tees, in April 1967. *Both PJR.*

CONSETT: Established in 1864, the Consett Iron Company drew its resources firstly from Cleveland and later from Spain, when the iron ore deposits at Carr House became worked-out. The Stanhope & Tyne Railway, the main transport system for the various works in the area, failed in late 1840 and the iron companies started planning alternative routes to keep supply and demand satisfied. Coal was obtained from Medomsley whilst limestone (needed for flux) came from Stanhope. In 1889, the Garesfield Colliery, its railway and staithes were taken over by the Consett company and eventually, by the end of the century, Derwenthaugh Quay was remodelled to meet the extra traffic demands. The Consett Iron Company's operations underpinned the whole system, but its furnaces were insatiable and the transport costs were enormous. Closure of the works and its busy railway artery eventually became inevitable and the furnaces were allowed to cool for the last time in 1983. The railway, so vital to Consett's one-time prosperity played a final sad role in its demise, for as the works was broken up, piece by piece, it was taken away by train, to the smelters of Sheffield. The last 25 loaded wagons came 'down the bank', heading for Sheffield, on Wednesday September 14 1983, leaving just five empty wagons in Mr. Page's coal sidings. These last vehicles were led away on September 30 1983 by Class 37 No. 37023, Tyne Driver Jack Lodge, who thereby entered the history books as he ended a railway mineral tradition of more than 149 years.

Above: Suitably decorated for the occasion, Riddles '9F' No. 92063 stands beneath the loading gantry at Tyne Dock, ready to work 'The Tyne Docker', the last steam-hauled ore train to Consett, on November 19 1966. No. 92063 was withdrawn before the end of the month and was subsequently scrapped by Thompson's, of Stockton on Tees, in April 1967. *John Dawson Collection.*

NORTHUMBERLAND

SUNILAWS: Far to the north, adjacent to the England-Scotland border, Sunilaws station was a small country outpost of the type almost extinct today. The 1911 Census recorded a possible passenger catchment of just 228 people! The station was located $4\frac{1}{2}$ miles east of Sprouston, where NER metals connected 'end on' with the 'auld enemy' — the North British Railway. Sunilaws disappeared from the railway passenger map on July 4 1955, eight years before our 'past' photograph (above) was taken. On Easter Monday 1963, LNER 'B1' 4—6—0 No. 61324 (of St. Margaret's shed) is passing with a branch line railtour comprised of five BR Mk. 1 coaches. *PJR.*

Right, upper: The sad spectacle greeting the photographer in recent times at Sunilaws. This picture was taken in July 1987. *PJR.*

Right, lower: The Anglo-Scottish border sign which was once a familiar landmark west of Sunilaws. The disappearance of lineside 'peripherals' like this has left our railways the poorer in character. *Bill Hampson.*

YEAVERING CROSS-ING: This very attractive spot is located north of Akeld, between Wooler and Coldstream, and the NER signalman at this location certainly worked in beautiful surroundings. The line from Alnwick was completed in 1887, and became a 'great way round' from Alnmouth to Berwick. The 'past' picture, on March 18 1961, shows Tweedmouth's Ivatt '2MT' 2—6—0 No. 46482 pausing at Yeavering with the daily Coldstream — Wooler pick-up goods. Pottering about with branch trains of this nature must have been a pleasant duty indeed for these railwaymen. The line survived until 1965, since when the signalbox masonry has been used as the basis for a private house. *Stuart Sellar/PJR.*

ALNWICK: Alnwick's fine station, built in the grand style to impress the Duke of Northumberland, opened on August 19 1850, starting life as the terminus of a short spur linked to the Newcastle & Berwick Railway. Alnwick was also connected to the Berwick — St. Boswells line at Coldstream, via an inland route via Whittingham, Wooler and Mindrum. Alnwick was served by almost 50 trains daily in 1912, but services declined rapidly after the First World War and the Coldstream passenger service ended on September 22 1930. The Alnwick — Alnmouth service survived much longer, the branch not closing until January 29 1968. In the 1950s, the steam-worked Alnmouth-Alnwick shuttle, normally in the charge of a Class D20 4—4—0 was a great attraction to NER locomotive enthusiasts. In the 1960s, the service was usually worked by 'K1' 2—6—0s, until DMUs took over in 1966. Our 'past' view (top) shows 'K1' No. 62025 waiting to leave the attractive terminus at Alnwick, bound for Alnmouth, on May 1 1965. *A.R. Thompson.*

Above: Alnwick station on February 25 1987, in use as a warehouse. *PJR.*

Right: The grandeur of Alnwick's attractive terminus is illustrated well by this atmospheric view of 'K1' 2—6—0 No. 62012, awaiting departure with a morning 'local' to Alnmouth, during 1964. *Malcolm Dunnett.*

REDESMOUTH: This junction, pictured (left, upper) on August 14 1955, was in the heart of Northumberland, some 30 miles north of Hexham. The western route (on the left) was constructed by the North British Railway in an attempt to provide an alternative to the NER's Anglo-Scottish route, by running from Edinburgh to Newcastle via Hawick, Redesmouth and Hexham. The easterly route (right) was built by the Wansbeck Valley Railway Company, as far as Scotsgap, supported by the NBR which completed the line to Redesmouth. The NBR wanted to gain another route into England, this time via the Blyth & Tyne route, to enter Newcastle via Morpeth, Newsham and Backworth. Redesmouth Junction, much like Riccarton Junction on the Waverley route, was extremely isolated, and since passenger traffic ended in 1956 nature has reclaimed the trackbed. The 'past' picture was taken from the window of a Hexham-Hawick train, running into the western platform, hauled by 'J21' 0—6—0 No. 65103. Loaded aboard the train on the right are field guns from the Vickers Armstrong factory at Elswick, awaiting transfer to the neighbouring military exercise area. Left, lower: The sad face of Redesmouth Junction in May 1987; the water tank building has been converted into a splendid country house, but the signalbox is becoming an eyesore, as a result of planning restrictions — a pity, for it is a splendid structure. *R. Payne/PJR.*

ROTHBURY: This little station, the terminus of the 13-miles NBR branch from Scotsgap, on the Morpeth-Redesmouth line, is an ideal subject for a railway modeller! Rothbury occupied no more than four acres and is pictured (above) in 1950, as 'J21' No. 65103 prepares to turn — and note that the turntable saves space by providing access to both loop and engine shed. The branch passenger service to Morpeth was withdrawn on September 15 1952, freight traffic continuing until 1963; the track was lifted in 1964. The modern view (right) shows Rothbury in February 1987, with animal mart pens now occupying the former station site.
F.W. Hampson/PJR.

RAILWAYS TO HEXHAM

STOCKSFIELD: When our 'past' picture of Stocksfield (overleaf) was received from Bob Payne, it was jokingly suggested that we try to track down the smiling passengers on the right. The *Newcastle Evening Chronicle* liked the idea and on June 12 1987 the photograph was published (see below) in an attempt to try and find the family. The phone did not cease ringing for the first two evenings after publication, with more than two dozen persons claiming to be absolutely certain that they were either in the picture, or they knew the people concerned! On the third evening, the name 'Younger' was mentioned for the second time and an earnest search began. Eventually, Mary Younger, (now Mrs. Logan) 11 years of age at the time of the 'past' picture, was found and she confirmed that the picture showed her parents with her on a summer afternoon church excursion to Redesmouth on August 17 1955.

We were delighted, but then a further 'bonus' phone call produced positive identification of Bill Collingwood

as the young fireman leaning from the cab of 'J21' 0—6—0 No. 65103. Sadly, upon talking to Mary Logan we learned that her parents had died, but she was overjoyed to have found this picture as a memento of a very happy occasion that she recalls in detail. After a few 'false starts', we eventually met at Stocksfield on July 3 1987 and awaited the arrival of Class 47 No. 47366 *Institute of Civil Engineers,* in charge of the Tyne — Hexham freight. We had arranged a special 'stop order' with the BR Public Relations department at Newcastle and we staged the modern picture shown overleaf (lower). Stocksfield signalbox has gone, but the station still presents a tidy, if not manicured face, as in the past — and note that the opposite platform has been shortened. A final coincidence was that Bill Collingwood, and J. Armstrong, the driver of the Hexham 'trip', had been colleagues at Tyne yard depot until Bill retired five years beforehand! This was an interesting and particularly enjoyable pair of pictures to research.

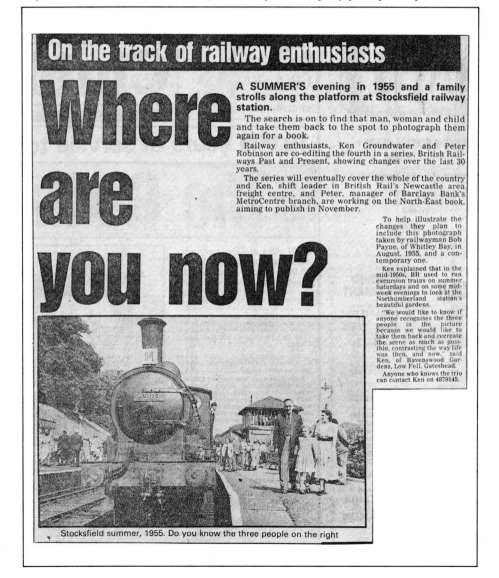

On the track of railway enthusiasts

Where are you now?

A SUMMER'S evening in 1955 and a family strolls along the platform at Stocksfield railway station.

The search is on to find that man, woman and child and take them back to the spot to photograph them again for a book.

Railway enthusiasts, Ken Groundwater and Peter Robinson are co-editing the fourth in a series, British Railways Past and Present, showing changes over the last 30 years.

The series will eventually cover the whole of the country and Ken, shift leader in British Rail's Newcastle area freight centre, and Peter, manager of Barclays Bank's MetroCentre branch, are working on the North-East book, aiming to publish in November.

To help illustrate the changes they plan to include this photograph taken by railwayman Bob Payne, of Whitley Bay, in August, 1955, and a contemporary one.

Ken explained that in the mid-1950s, BR used to run excursion trains on summer Saturdays and on some midweek evenings to look at the Northumberland station's beautiful gardens.

"We would like to know if anyone recognises the three people in the picture because we would like to take them back and recreate the scene as much as possible, contrasting the way life was then, and now," said Ken, of Ravenswood Gardens, Low Fell, Gateshead.

Anyone who knows the trio can contact Ken on 4879145.

Stocksfield summer, 1955. Do you know the three people on the right

Above & right: Footplateman Bill Collingwood and Tynesider Mary Logan at Stocksfield, on the Newcastle-Carlisle line, in 1955 and 1987, accompanied respectively by 'J21' 0—6—0 No. 65103 and Class 47 No. 47366 *Institute of Civil Engineers.* **See also previous page.** *Bob Payne/PJR.*

HEXHAM had an early place on the railway map, on the 1835 Newcastle — Carlisle route, the first cross-country passenger line in England. The station is well worth visiting in the 1980s, for it still provides a glimpse of genuine rural railway charm and our pictures show the east end of the station which on March 18 1987 (above) still had a thriving goods yard, to the left of this field of view. The most recent additional traffic dated from July 1 1987, when the area Civil Engineer at Newcastle transferred his ballast loading operations to Hexham, from Belford Quarry. The depot also deals in wood, resin, food flavourings and occasionally farming equipment. The 1872 footbridge has lost its roof, but the scene has been enhanced by the resiting of the fine NER lattice-post signal on the right, and the short semaphore on the left. Class 47 No. 47569 was in charge of a three-coach 'Pacer' replacement duty (the 1237 Carlisle-Newcastle). The 'past' picture (top) taken in August 1959, features Class B16 4—6—0 No. 61459, a relative stranger to this area, en route home to Selby, via York, in charge of a Heads of Ayr — Newcastle train. *Both: PJR.*

BORDER COUNTIES JUNCTION, NEAR HEXHAM: This junction was the point at which the single track Border Counties Railway diverged northwards to Redesmouth from the Newcastle-Carlisle route. The NBR bought the Border Counties line, intending to connect its existing Hawick-Carlisle (Waverley) route to the BCR at Redesmouth. This move gave the NBR a foothold at Hexham, but the NER acted promptly and bought the Newcastle-Carlisle route to prevent further incursions by the NBR into NER territory. Freight traffic over the BCR route was always disappointing, and passenger business was little better — and hardly surprising, when a 'fast' train from Newcastle — Edinburgh took five hours via this circuitous 42-miles route. Thus, passenger traffic between Border Counties Junction and Riccarton Junction ended in 1956. Our 'past' picture (above) shows BR Class 3MT 2—6—0 No. 77011 approaching the Junction on October 13 1956, actually the last day of regular services. *Bill Hampson.*

Right, upper: The site of Border Counties Junction, on March 18 1987. The bridge piers still survive, but the rural tranquillity of the middle distance is bisected nowadays by the Hexham by-pass. The railway cottage adjacent to the trackbed still stands, although much-extended. *PJR.*

Right, lower: An interesting eastward view of the Junction and its highly distinctive signalbox. The right-hand signal on the triple bracket was for the Allendale branch, closed to passengers on September 22 1930, and freight in 1952. *J.W. Armstrong.*

HALTWHISTLE: This station, on the Newcastle-Carlisle route, was the junction for the Alston branch, which against all odds outlived its freight role by 11 years, the passenger service surviving until May 3 1976. The 'past' picture (top) shows Haltwhistle, looking east, on October 27 1956, as 'B1' 4—6—0 No. 61239 departs with the 12.25pm Newcastle-Carlisle service. On the right, an Alston train is awaiting departure. This was a most attractive country junction station with its own goods yard, which in 1956 still appeared to be quite busy. The modern view of Haltwhistle (above) on March 14 1987, reveals that only minimal rationalisation had occurred, despite the loss of the Alston branch, and the station still retained much of its previous character. The signalbox survives and the goods yard is still in use for the despatch of 'Kilfrost' a de-icing solution used by the railways since 1938, first on Tyneside and later on the Southern Region, to keep conductor rails clear. Incredibly, the locomotive water columns survive, nearly two decades after the end of steam traction! They would be a useful acquisition by one of our privately operated steam railways. *Robert Leslie/PJR.*

SOUTH GOSFORTH station, at the lower point of a large triangle in the north west Newcastle suburbs, originated on the Blyth & Tyne main line to New Bridge Street in 1864. In the 1960s, this location became popular for the occasional passenger trains of a very important nature, when the Royal Train was stabled overnight, during visits to the region. Above: On March 23 1967, gleaming two-tone green liveried Brush Type 4 (later) Class 47) No. D 1999 (now 47297) passes South Gosfort in charge of the resplendent mixed BR and LNER Roya Train. Below: A rather different scene, almost 20 year to the day later, in 1987, with South Gosforth now staging post on the Tyne & Wear 'Metro' system. Thi station is used as a convenient point for crew changes o the 'Metro' trains, which operate for 16 hours each day *KG/PJR.*

PONTELAND: The Gosforth & Ponteland Light Railway began trading on June 1 1905, along the proposed track-bed of the Blyth & Tyne 'South Northumberland Railway', originally planned in 1860 to reach Scots Gap, via Kenton Walbottle and Whorlton. Traffic of a light nature to then-rural Gosforth and Ponteland justified a light railway order (which also helped minimise expenses) but the NER subsequently shelved plans to electrify the route into the North Tyne loop system. Our 'past' picture (above) shows Ponteland station, apparently shortly after opening, with a 'push-pull' train comprised of an 0—4—4T and two coaches. The branch closed in June 1929, but other parts of the route are still in use by 'Metro' trains running between South Gosforth and Kenton Bank Foot. The modern view (below) shows the original Ponteland station site on February 16 1987, now occupied by 'Co-Op' offices. *Newcastle City Libraries/PJR.*

ELSWICK: Robert Bell, the LNER's Assistant General Manager, said in 1929 that: "nowhere are trade and transport more closely connected than on the north-east coast, and to the heavy industries the railways are indispensable — in fact, it is easier to get into some of the larger works by river or rail than by road." He could easily have had Elswick in mind, for in the three miles between the Scotswood Road (immortalised by folk song) and the river were packed more manufacturers than were either practical or convenient for the space available. Nevertheless, this was indicative of early industrial Tyneside at its busiest, and few local residents could sleep peacefully at nights during the continual 'din' created by the steam hammers, crashing steel plates and general 'fire and brimstone' of the seve days-a-week industrial bustle. There was the Elswi lead works and its 'shot tower' (demolished in 1969), Gas Works (made redundant by natural ga Richardson's Tannery (closed in 1971) and final Armstrong's Elswick works. In 1847, Willi Armstrong had started a small factory maki hydraulic equipment, but the Crimean War turned attention to armaments and, since that time, business developed rapidly into the Vickers Armstro complex now known throughout the world. Our p picture (below) shows Elswick station circa 1920, wit train of mixed stock on the left, whilst on the down si is a Carlisle express. *K.L. Taylor Collection.*

Right: Elswick station site on March 5 1986, following closure (January 2 1967) and demolition, as the BR light engine arrives to collect the empty tar wagons (bound for Stanlow) from Jobling Purser's pitch sidings at the rather ironically-named Paradise Works! Around 20 tanks per week are delivered to the sidings, to provide the raw material for road surfacing. Other traffic latterly using the line was to Stella North Power Station, which is now closed, the railway terminating nowadays 200 yards west of Elswick. *KG.*

WCASTLE CENTRAL
EST END): The west
d of Central station
sumed its fully de-
loped form with the
mpletion in 1906 of the
ng Edward VII Bridge.
 these pictures, the
ML diverges immedia-
y left across the Tyne,
d the station is behind
e photographer, whilst
utes to the west
ntinued along the
erbank, past the
otswood Bridge, where
e South Tyne route to
aydon crossed the
er. This trio of views
ows three phases in the
velopment of this
portant junction.

NEWCASTLE CENTRAL

Above: Leaving Platform 8 at Newcastle Central on July 23 1937 is Gresley 'A4' No. 2509 *Silver Link,* at the head of the 1.55pm Edinburgh — King's Cross service. The locomotive is passing beneath the magnificent gantry of NER lower quadrant semaphores and approaching No. 3 signalbox, which had 211 levers, worked by a Supervisor, three signalmen and a group of telephone and train register 'booking' lads. *W.B. Greenfield (Courtesy NELPG).*

Left, upper: A similar viewpoint on July 25 1964; the signalbox and the superb gantry have given way to simpler colour light signalling, but the Forth Goods depot building still stands in the 'Y' of the junction. Leaving Platform 8 with a troop train bound for Carlisle is Gresley 'V2' 2—6—2 No. 60895, whilst on the left, Peppercorn Class A1 'Pacific' No. 60124 *Kenilworth* takes water at the head of an empty stock train. *Malcolm Dunnett.*

Left, lower: The clock is advanced another 23 years, and by May 31 1987 there has been much rationalisation and clearance; the track layout is much simpler and the Forth Goods Depot was demolished in 1972/3. Visible in the distance is the Redheugh Bridge. The HST was leaving Platform 9, heading for King's Cross. *PJR.*

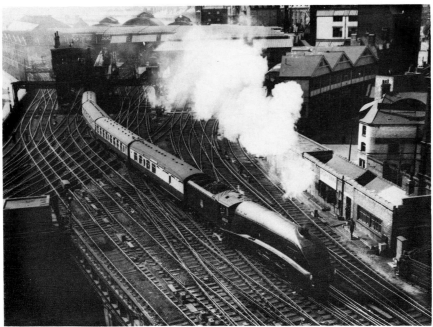

NEWCASTLE CENTRA
This famous location, viewed from the Ke tower, has always bee popular with railwa photographers. It is on fitting that the 10.00a from King's Cross — th famous 'Flying Scotsma — should appear with these pages, and the tra is depicted (left) durin 1959, leaving Newcast in the charge of No. 6002 *Kingfisher.* This was Haymarket locomotiv and a regular visitor Tyneside. Sadly th locomotive ended i days in the north east, fo following withdrawal September 1966, the 'A was scrapped by Hugh Bolckow, North Blyth February 1967. At th time, Newcastle Central No. 1 signalbox still s astride the station throa although it was awaitin demolition. *M. Halbe Collection.*

Right: A similar viewpoint in July 1978, as a Class 55 'Deltic' threads the junction with a Kings Cross — Edinburgh express. The removal of the signal gantry and the cutting back of the station roof (see also rear cover) created a more 'open' vista from the Keep. Note the various DMUs on the right in use on local services. *PJR.*

38

NEWCASTLE DIAMOND CROSSING: Central station evolved from plans made by Robert Stephenson in 1843 for the adaptation of the site (much of which was formerly owned by the Newcastle & Carlisle Railway) into a joint facility, with access from Gateshead and the south via a proposed new Tyne bridge. In 1848, a temporary wooden bridge was opened, prior to the completion of Stephenson's famous twin-level bridge, of which the upper deck was used by trains, the lower by road vehicles. By 1850, this well-known diamond junction, with lines coming in from the left from the high level bridge to run into the new enlarged station, was complete. Below: A view of the junction circa 1900, by which time all trains from the south were arriving via the new bridge, and nearly all required a locomotive change. This created a scene of frenzied activity and the elevated signalbox, completed in 1909 to cope with increasing traffic, was provided with a 'flying bridge' to enable a pointsman to shout and ask locomotive crews their train numbers and destinations, before replying with their route details. The NER signal gantry is quite breathtaking in its complexity. Locomotives in view include (from the left) Fletcher Class 398 0—6—0 No. 32, Class 'R' 'Greyhound' 4—4—0 (later Class D20) No. 2108, and Class 'E' 0—6—0T (later Class J71) No. 969. *Newcastle City Libraries.*

Left: After the withdrawal of the popular 'Deltics' in January 1981, the impressive HST sets were left in complete mastery of the ECML, and on November 10 1986, a down express is seen leaving Newcastle. By this time, platforms 1-3 had been closed and the tracks lifted to make room for the inevitable car park. Both passenger and freight trains can be seen — on the left of the station a coal container train is snaking past. Notwithstanding the rationalisation of this famous junction, any rail enthusiast will derive much enjoyment from spending a couple of hours on the battlements of the Keep. As this book went to press, Newcastle was preparing for further significant change, for electrification will take the ECML into the 1990s — though one casualty will of course be this uncluttered view. *KG.*

NEWCASTLE FORTH GOODS: The site of Newcastle Forth Goods Station, occupied today by a BR engineers depot, as illustrated here on August 31 1987. Only the curving northern wall and some truncated platform stonework remain as solitary reminders of the past. Note the King Edward VII Bridge approach, in the background, built in 1906. *PJR.*

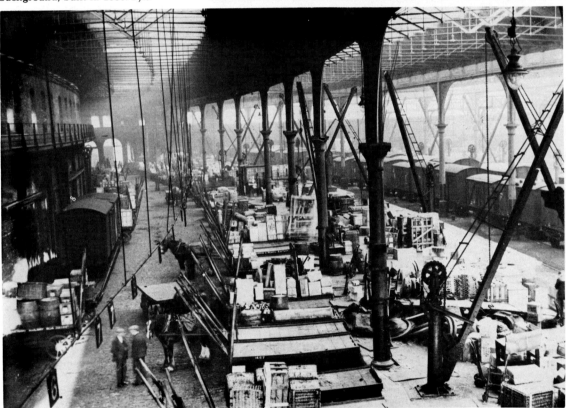

Above: A similar viewpoint circa 1930, with the goods depot hard at work. Note the very large number of handcranes, and the King Edward VII Bridge, dimly visible in the background. 'Forth Goods' was developed on a site originally acquired by the Newcastle & Carlisle Railway in 1843, in the hope that it would become the major westward-facing passenger station for Scotland, via the route to Border Counties Junction, Riccarton and the Waverley route. When Newcastle Central station was eventually constructed further east, as a joint station, the Forth site was developed as the MCR's goods terminal, the first depot, opening on June 2 1854. However, in early NER days it became clear that larger, more efficient goods-handling facilities were required and on March 3 1871, the large goods station illustrated began trading. At first, only traffic from the west was handled, but by 1874 coverage was extended to cover all points of the compass. This sort of goods handling is a far cry indeed from the Speedlink and block-load working of today! *Newcastle City Library.*

NEWCASTLE QUAYSIDE: The overall scene here has changed little, although railway activity ceased in 1969. The 'past' view (above) shows the quay pilot for the day (supplied by Heaton MPD), Class J72 0—6—0T No. 69024, in 1961, during a move between the Copenhagen Wharf and the quayside dock yard, in the background. Traffic on Newcastle quay dwindled rapidly during the 1960s and closure followed in 1969. No. 69024 was scrapped in September 1963, but sister engine No. 69023 *Joem* survives on the North Yorkshire Moors Railway. *A.R. Thompson Collection.*

Above: By June 5 1987, the industrial skyline in the left distance has changed, but much else remains as it was in 1961: the buildings on the right are still there and the dockside rails have escaped the scrap merchant. However, business is now concentrated lower down the River Tyne, either at North Shields or at more convenient deep-water facilities on the River Tees, or at Hull. The Newcastle quayside branch was well-known for its steeple-cab electric locomotives, one of which survives as a member of the National Collection. *A.R. Thompson.*

MANORS NORTH: Located east of Newcastle Central, Manors North started life as the New Bridge terminus of the Blyth & Tyne Railway, but was converted into a through station in 1909, when it assumed the form illustrated in our 'past' picture (top). It chiefly served commuters arriving daily in the east end of the city centre, but here we see 'V3' 2—6—2T No. 67620 departing from Platform 1 towards Ponteland with an enthusiasts tour on September 29 1963. The station lay derelict for several years, the site bisected immediately behind the camera by a motorway interchange. The modern picture (above) shows the scene in March 1987, with only the truncated platforms remaining in situ.
A.R. Thompson/PJR.

EAST OF NEWCASTLE

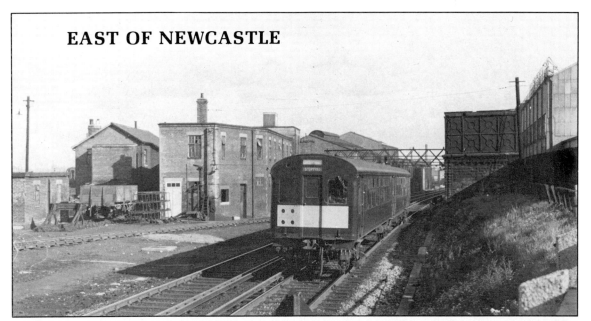

HEATON JUNCTION: The railway at this point originated in the late 1830s, with the opening on June 19 1839 of the Newcastle & North Shields Railway, running from Carliol Square via All Saints, north of Byker Hill and through Heaton to the coast. Absorption by the Newcastle & Berwick Railway followed in 1847 and with the completion of the adjacent junction and routes to the north, the stage was set for Heaton to develop into a railway centre of major importance. Our past picture (top) shows one of the green-liveried two-car articulated electric EMUs (introduced by the LNER in 1937) at Heaton on September 25 1965. These once-familiar trains swayed along with their destination blinds proclaiming 'Express', 'Stopping' or (especially exciting for the children!) 'Coast'. Although it might at first be difficult to believe, the modern picture (above) shows the same scene on July 7 1987 — the large industrial building on the right positively identifies the location. This slightly realigned route is today part of the Tyne & Wear 'Metro' system, with the latest generation of suburban electric traction now serving Tynesiders. *Both: KG.*

WALLSEND: Located on the early Newcastle & North Shields (1839) route, Wallsend was busy for most of its working life for BR, carrying shipyard commuters and shoppers en route to and from Newcastle. The station goods shed was also kept busy with a variety of merchandise until 1949, by which time the concentration process for this business was well under way. Goods sundries were therefore transferred to the Forth Goods Depot (see page 40) and for a time heavier goods traffic was transferred to nearby Carville, on the adjacent Riverside branch. On March 29 1967 (top) goods trip 8P17 is pictured en route to the coast from Tyne Yard in the charge of a Clayton Type 1 (later Class 17) No. D 8594. Wallsend commenced operations as part of the Tyne & Wear 'Metro' system on May 9 1983 and the modern picture (above) shows the modernised station with new canopies and shortened platforms, on March 24 1987. *Ian S. Carr/PJR.*

PERCY MAIN LOCOMOTIVE SHED: This depot, and the neighbouring wagon and locomotive workshops, were built by the Blyth & Tyne Railway in the mid-19th Century and eventually looked after 37 locomotives, 77 coaches, and 56 goods wagons. The complex also maintained more than 3,000 chaldron wagons used for moving Northumberland coal down to the staithes at Northumberland Dock on the River Tyne. From the 1870s, the works was chiefly used for scrapping old NER engines, until the turn of the century, when this work was concentrated at Darlington; however, intermittent scrapping continued at Percy Main on an 'overflow' basis until 1920. In later years the shed housed many class J27 0—6—0s and a small fleet of diesel shunters. On February 28 1965, the steam allocation was moved, and of the shed's 14 remaining 'J27s', 10 went to South Blyth and 3 to North Blyth. Unfortunately, No. 65780, pictured (below) at Percy Main on July 31 1953, was not amongst them; it was withdrawn in April 1959. On February 27 1966, the remaining diesel allocation was transferred to Gateshead and Percy Main shed closed. All trace of the railway has since disappeared, as shown in the 'present' picture (lower). A new housing development now occupies part of the site. Both pictures were taken from the route of the former Cramlington Wagonway. *Bill Hampson/A.R. Thompson.*

TYNE COMMISSION QUAY: This was a private, chiefly goods branch running to the River Tyne, from Percy Main North, and best known to many people for its named train from Kings Cross for the Norwegian Boat connection — 'The Norseman', which arrived at the Quay mid-evening. A note in the working timetable for 1939 stated: "The timings for passenger and empty trains to and from TCQ may be altered as necessary by the Station Master at Newcastle Central", also adding: "empty trains from TCQ to Heaton Sidings may convey passengers to Walker Gate when required." In the same year, two passenger trains ran on Thursdays-only from the quayside at 0713 and 1340, with five fish train paths, as required at 1520, 1730, 1845, 1940 and 2145. Doubtless there were occasions when all five trains ran, probably behind Heaton 'V2' 2—6—2s. Opened for traffic on June 15 1928, the last day of service on the branch was May 2 1970. Above: On May 31 1954, Class V1 No. 67646 is raising steam ready to work the 0840 to Newcastle, whilst sister engine No. 67651 will follow with the 0910 service, eventually bound for King's Cross. Both trains are standing in the carriage sidings where trains were held prior to drawing forward and reversing into the Bergen Line terminal and platform, to the left of this view. *R.K. Taylor.*

Above: Taken in April 1987, the modern view shows the current link-span (centre background) used for 'Ro-Ro' operations by North Sea ferries steaming under the DFDS Danish Flag. The quayside rails, embedded in concrete, lie unused today whilst on the left is an oil rig under repair. In the distance are the shipyard cranes of the declining Tyneside shipbuilding industry. *A.R. Thompson.*

WILLINGTON QUAY: This outpost on the North Tyneside Riverside branch, served chiefly as a shipyard workers halt on a line of primarily industrial character. Services commenced in 1879 and its last surviving section, from St. Peters to Byker Junction retained to serve a scrapyard at St. Peters, closed on Friday September 25 1987. Our past illustration (left, upper) shows the last regular passenger train about to leave Willington Quay on July 20 1973. Under the decaying awning, a hand-chalked notice reads: "No more waiting here after today." The first section to be lifted was between NE Marine sidings and the junction at Percy Main. In 1987 (left, lower) the trackbed was desolate and abandoned, only the Howard-Doris construction sheds in the distance providing a positive link between the two pictures. *Ian S. Carr/PJR.*

BACKWORTH: This station, at a northern point on the North Tyne loop, served its farming village and parts of neighbouring Earsden. The past scene (right) in July 1966, looks towards Benton, with the Backworth wagonway bridge spanning the platforms. This NCB line closed on August 27 1969, when traffic for the Docks was re-routed via BR metals and the Blyth and Tyne Line. The North Tyne Metro-Cammell electric trains of the type illustrated here, introduced in 1937, ran for a further year after this picture was taken. The train shown is just arriving from Newcastle, after which it will run via the coast, returning to Newcastle via Heaton. *KG.*

Above: Backworth station closed on June 13 1977, but the railway survives as part of Newcastle's 'Metro' system, opened in August 1980. The station site has been widened to allow a BR mineral line to run alongside the Metro tracks. This picture shows the view from the same location in July 1987 as a Metro train approaches, collecting its power from 1500 volts DC overhead catenary, rather than third rail, as in the 'past' scene. *KG.*

GATESHEAD & SOUTH TYNESIDE

GATESHEAD, KING EDWARD BRIDGE JUNCTION: This view, looking east towards Gateshead locomotive shed, was often the scene of spectacular scenes in steam days, as heavy trains for the south struggled over the steeply graded curves. It was particularly interesting when up expresses were diverted via the High Level Bridge. Top: No. 60005 *Sir Charles Newton* storms past King Edward Bridge Junction Signal Box with the 4.30pm semi-fast to Leeds on May 27 1962. 'No. 5' had been on duty that day as Gateshead's main line pilot, and was allocated for a 'run out' on this fairly leisurely job, which was planned to bring the Gateshead engine home in readiness for Monday's more demanding duties. The current scene in May 1987 (above) reveals a degree of rationalisation of the track layout and the loss of the signalbox, as a 'Pacer' unit passes, bound for Carlisle, with the 1928 departure from Newcastle. *Both: A.R. Thompson.*

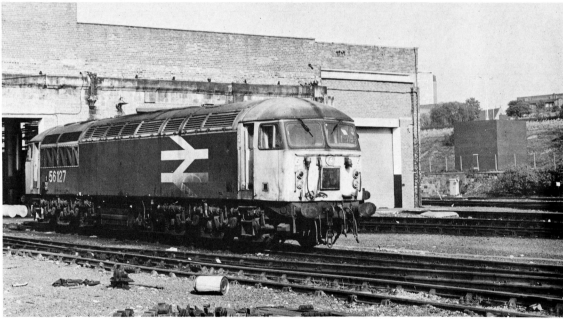

GATESHEAD GREENFIELD locomotive shed evolved in rather piecemeal fashion on a site which was barely suitable for the purpose, but even so, at its zenith, housed and maintained more than 150 locomotives. The developing railways of the area 'imprisoned' the shed site in a web of steel rails, and it was a tribute to the depot staff over the years that late-running was rarely booked against locomotives being late 'off-shed' — for it could be perilously easy for engines required for service to become 'trapped' and therefore delayed in the cramped shed and yard. Tight and skilled control of engine movements and stabling was needed. Top: On a beautiful summer evening in 1963, stabled around the turntable are (left to right): 'J72' 0—6—0T No. 69014; 'V3' 2—6—2T No. 67643; 'K1' 2—6—0 No. 62028; 'J72' 0—6—0T No. 69005; 'V3' 2—6—2T No. 67653 and 'V3' 2—6—2T No. 67636. This turntable was 'squeezed in' between the maintenance shed and the King Edward VII Bridge approach. *PJR.*

Above: The same viewpoint in March 1987, with Class 56 No. 56127 awaiting its next turn of duty. The turntable pit has been filled to create more space in the still-cramped shed yard, whilst in the background, the terraced housing has been demolished in favour of an urban motorway. The depot is scheduled to close in 1988. *PJR.*

GATESHEAD EAST & WEST STATIONS: This distinctive junction station was located at the convergence of routes at the southern end of Newcastle's High Level Bridge, immediately behind the camera in this view of Gateshead East. Gateshead West, opened in 1868, with its similarly curving track, was off to the right of this view, linked to the Team Valley route. The West station closed to passengers on November 1 1965, and was used latterly only as an occasional station and a parcels/pigeon traffic collection point for the morning Newcastle — Red Bank parcels service. Gateshead East, pictured here (below) lasted until 1981 when its role was taken over by the 'Metro' system. The 'past' view shows Gateshead East in 1954, as an 'A8' 4—6—2T draws in bunker-first with a Sunderland — Newcastle train, whilst in the modern view of the same location on July 7 1987, the decaying station is shorn of its arched roof and curved platforms. *J.W. Armstrong/KG.*

WARDLEY: Whilst most of our pairs of pictures show changes of around 30 years in interval, this page illustrates just how quickly a once-busy location can fall into disuse and dereliction. This is Wardley sidings (above) the interchange point for traffic running between BR metals and the Bowes Railway, the private system run by the Bowes-Lyon family, of which today's Queen Elizabeth the Queen Mother is a member. Th 'past' picture (above) shows the exchange sidings i 1983, with plenty of 21-ton bottom-discharging hoppe in use. These wagons were very characteristic of nort east coal train operation, and were designed for rapi 'teeming' (discharge) into dockside colliers. Class 37 N 37068 is waiting to leave the yard. *David Allen.*

Above: Wardley sidings finally closed in late 1985, and when the 'present' picture was taken, on July 9 1987, th sidings were still intact, although abandoned and overgrown, and with the shunters cabin boarded and awaiting th demolition gang. This is indeed a sad epitaph to the end of conventional coal hopper traffic in the north east. K(

OUTH SHIELDS (ST. HILDA COLLIERY): This once-usy port-and-mining town, mid-way between Tyne ock and the Tyne estuary, grew rapidly during the late 9th century, the 1861 population of 100,000 tripling by he early 1900s. Railways were built not for passengers, ut for moving coal from the pitheads to dockside. St. iilda's Colliery was a focal point on the town's complex ineral network, and an indication of the intensity of idustrial activity at this time is recorded by a ntemporary 'Murray's Handbook for Travellers' hich described Eastern Durham as: "blackened by smoke of its numerous collieries, which poisons vegetation and overspreads the heavens like a pall". Our 'past' view of St. Hilda's Colliery (top) circa 1920, shows a great deal of detail. Opened in 1844, the Colliery railway was eventually electrified using a catenary system and electric locomotives. The modern picture (above) taken in July 1987, reveals that whilst the colliery has been swept away, the 1844 winding house still stands as an escape facility from Westoe pit, which in hte late 1980s is still using part of the electrified railway. *North of England Open Air Museum/KG.*

SOUTH SHIELDS: The first railway to South Shields was built by the Stanhope & Tyne company, from Consett, via Washington, in 1834. This company's first station was about 50 yards beyond the view shown here, but was relocated to the position illustrated in 1879, following expansion of the local system. Our 'past' picture (below) illustrates a Sunderland train standing at South Shields, beneath the impressive overall roof, in the charge of Class G5 0—6—2T No. 67247. Th station closed in June 1981, but in March 1984 this rou became part of the Tyne & Wear PTE rapid trans system, with a new station built 100 yards south of th site. The modern picture (lower) was taken on July 1987, since when parts of the remaining station buildi have also been demolished. *W.A. Camwell/KG.*

MARSDEN GROTTO: Located half-way between South Shields and Whitburn, on the North Sea coast, Marsden Grotto was also approximately the half-way point of a very short private colliery railway — The South Shields Marsden & Whitburn Colliery Railway. In March 1885 a workers passenger service commenced later known as 'The Marsden Rattler'. In 1947 the NCB took over the system and its passenger service continued until November 1953, the line thereafter being used only for coal traffic; it became redundant after 1968 with the closure of Whitburn Colliery. Our 'past' picture (above) is extremely interesting in depicting a vintage NER train running on a private passenger line, on August 2 1949. The 0—6—0 in charge was built at Gateshead Works in 1889 as a Class 'C' compound designed by T.W. Worsdell. Originally NER No. 996, the 0—6—0 soon became No. 1509, and was converted to simple operation in 1904. In August 1935, the engine was sold to the Harton Coal Company, becoming HCC No. 6; it was scrapped in March 1951. Left: The same scene, pictured on July 9 1987. The trolley bus turning circle survives as a lay-by, but of the colliery railway no trace remains. *William J. Skillern/ KG.*

PELAW JUNCTION: Located east of Gateshead on the South bank of the River Tyne, the railway at Pelaw dates from 1839, and this fascinating trio of pictures examines three types of electric passenger trains which have served the people of Newcastle. Although the North Tyneside loop electrification had been commenced in 1904, electrification of the Newcastle — Pelaw — South Shields services was only proposed in the years before the First World War, and the scheme was not complete until 1938. Our oldest picture (opposite page, top) depicts Pelaw in 1938, with a NER six-car set of rather American appearance. New Metro-Cammell sets introduced in 1937 to replace this NER stock worked until 1955 (see page 48) when BR introduced new Eastleigh-built SR trains into service on Tyneside, as illustrated in our intermediate view (opposite page, lower). This picture was taken in 1958 at Pelaw, which had gained an overbridge since the previous picture was taken. The Eastleigh sets returned to the Southern Region (where in the late 1980s they are still in use) in 1963, when DMUs took over their duties in Newcastle. This pattern continued until early 1970, when BR made known its difficulties in maintaining the Newcastle suburban service with ageing DMUs, and in the face of falling receipts and increasing vandalism of its property, Newcastle's transport authority and local councillors met the challenge 'head-on' and following the report of a working party established in 1971 the parliamentary Bill to permit the creation of Tyneside Metropolitan Railway received royal assent in July 1973. The 'Metro' incorporates 27 miles of former BR routes, with a further eight miles (including four miles underground) serving Central Newcastle, and the new trains started running from August 11 1980. The Pelaw — South Shields section began operations in late March 1984, although there was initially no service from Pelaw as a result of a shortage of finance for station reconstruction. Pelaw was reprieved however, and this new station opened on September 15 1985, an official ceremony following on September 23. The station is pictured (above) on February 8 1987. The 'Metro' train shown is carrying an incorrect destination display, and is actually leaving in the Newcastle direction, from South Shields. This system, with a total route mileage of 35, actually features four separate operational routes: No. 1, Bank Foot — South Shields; No. 2, Benton — Heworth; No. 3, St. James — Heworth; No. 4, St. James — North Shields. The service is provided by Metro-Cammell two-car six-axle articulated units capable of carrying 84 passengers. The single-manned twin units weigh slightly over 38 tons, have a maximum speed of 50mph and are 91ft 3in in length; no buffing gear is fitted and the central couplings are operated by the driver. The cars are maintained at South Gosforth.

W.B. Greenfield (Courtesy NELPG)/R. Payne/PJR.

DUNSTON: This station, west of Gateshead has had a chequered career, but its recent history has provided a very positive aspect of railway development. The route was proposed just after 1900, when plans were in hand for the construction of the King Edward VII Bridge (completed in 1906), required to streamline operations at Central station and enable Robert Stephenson's High Level Bridge to help cope with the large amount of north-south traffic. In order that traffic from Hexham and the West could run directly to South Tyneside and East Durham, the Dunston extension was opened in 1907, linking the Newcastle-Carlisle route, near West Dunston, with the 1868 main Team Valley Route, at Bensham. Dunston station opened on New Year's Day 1909, and provided the NER's shortest branch service, to Newcastle, a distance of just over two miles. In 1918, its staff had all departed for Flanders and it was closed, only to re-open again with enlisted women workers. In the face of stiff competition from local tramways, Dunston closed again in 1926, but fortunately, from May 4 1982, Carlisle passenger trains were permanently re-routed via Dunston and the station reopened once again in 1984. Our oldest 'past' picture (top, left) shows Dunston station site in derelict condition in 1955, passenger services having ended on May 4 1926. The intermediate view (top, right) depicts the cleared site in 1980 whilst the modern picture (above) shows the rejuvenated station on March 11 1987, with 'Pacer' No. 143014 forming the 1257 Middlesbrough-Carlisle service. Note that the original goods shed, albeit minus side-awning, still survives. *A.J. Wickens/KG/PJR.*

NORWOOD: Norwood Coking plant, sited just off the Dunston Extension railway between Bensham and Dunston, was typical of Newcastle's one-time inner city industry. The coke works was fully established by 1912 on this site, between the Team and Tyne Valleys, as a focal point and crossroads 'twixt road and rail. In its latter days, the Works was a 'Mecca' for industrial steam locomotive enthusiasts, as it frequently received redundant engines 'cascaded' from other National Smokeless Fuels depots. Above: On April 1 1964, RSH 0—4—0ST (Works No. 7799 built in 1954) gets to grips with a rake of BR 21-ton coal hoppers. *A.R. Thompson.*

Left: Norwood Works closed in 1984, and in the 'present' view, taken on December 26 1986, the site is being redeveloped to host the 1990 National Garden Festival. Only the chimney in the middle distance links this pair of pictures. *PJR.*

LOW FELL JUNCTION, south of Gateshead, was the point at which the Anglo-Scottish main line was joined from the west, at the turn of the century, by the Dunston staithes extension railway to create a four-track main line. This became something of a bottleneck, with queues forming of up to four miles in length, a problem which was subsequently erased by the extension of the four-track section to Ouston, in the 1940s. From 1963, instead of easing the path of mineral trains, the junction became the point where freight for Tyne Yard accessed the slow lines. Below: On May 11 1940, 'A4' No. 2509 *Silver Link* accelerates past with the up 'Flying Scotsman'. Low Fell station, immediately behind the camera, was mainly used by local services on the Newcastle — Birtley — Consett route, but suffered from competing tram services and closure followed on April 7 1952. *W.B. Greenfield (Courtesy NELPG).*

Right: On June 5 1987, Class 37 No. 37429 passes Low Fell with a Newcastle — Bristol parcels service. High-rise blocks of flats now breach the distant skyline, whilst at Low Fell itself, new buildings border the lineside. The picture once again provides a graphic illustration of how surviving railways are becoming increasingly 'closed in' by trees and bushes. *PJR.*

DOXFORD'S SHIPYARD: This famous shipyard retained steam traction until 1971, with these unique 0—4—0 crane tanks built by Robert Stephenson & Hawthorns. The yard was west of the Queen Alexandra Bridge, which was rather a white elephant — it was short-lived in railway service and is still maintained today by BR, with only a road deck in use! The 'past' picture (below) was taken on April 24 1966, when five of the crane tanks were 'on shed'. The two leading engines are *Millfield* (right) and *Roker* (left). Also housed here was a conventional locomotive by the name of *General*, an 0—4—0ST built by Peckett in 1944. *A.R. Thompson.*

SUNDERLAND
&
DISTRICT

Left: The Doxford engine shed site on June 5 1987, with the Queen Alexandra Bridge still standing in the background. The engine shed area has completely changed, following clearance and landscaping as a Doxford's employees park. Note the ships ventilators, rather sadly in use today as rubbish bins. *A.R. Thompson.*

SUNDERLAND CENTRAL station was completed by the NER as late as 1879 when the Monkwearmouth Junction Railway linked Monkwearmouth with Ryhope Grange via the Wearmouth Bridge and two tunnels. It superseded the earlier Fawcett Street and Hendon stations and put Sunderland on a through route served by long distance passenger trains. Sunderland's two island platforms were below street-level with an overall roof (which was damaged by a bomb during the Second World War), and passenger exits at both north and south ends. The view of 'Deltic' No. D9012 *Crepello* (above, left) leaving with a London train on June 28 1964 shows the second south passenger entrance, opened in 1953 when the remains of the overall roof were removed. Following the withdrawal of local passenger services to Durham, South Shields and East Hartlepool, rationalisation of the layout at Sunderland took place in 1965 when the line to Fawcett Street junction was severed and a new signalbox built further south. All passenger traffic was thereafter concentrated on the east side island, with a parcels loop at one face of the west island. New station buildings were constructed at the south end and the north end buildings were closed; a Littlewoods store now occupies the site. The August 13 1985 picture (above, right) shows No. 56078 passing the simplified layout with a southbound train of MGR 'empties'. During 1987 the parcels loop was removed and this area was being enclosed by the Waterloo Way shopping development. *Both: Ian S. Carr.*

NORTH DOCK BRANCH (SUNDERLAND) About one mile long, the North Dock branch of 1839 diverged from the Brandling Junction Railway's main line to the south of the present Seaburn station. The branch was worked by locomotives, though stationary engines were the rule for wagon haulage on the steep grades at the seaward end. Sadly, North Dock became overshadowed in importance by Hudson's South Dock complex across the River Wear (which was not bridged by rail until 1879). The 1963 picture (right, upper) shows 'J27' 0—6—0 No. 65887 running round its pick-up goods train at Fulwell Crossing, a couple of years before the branch was abandoned, track singling having been carried out in the meantime. A portion of the trackbed adjacent to the bus depot (right, lower) was used until 1987 to accommodate Sunderland Busways vehicles. *Both: Ian S. Carr.*

WASHINGTON: Washington's first station was on the Stanhope & Tyne Railway (of 1834, from Stanhope to South Shields) but passenger services on this route ceased east of Washington in 1853 and west of Washington in 1869. The later station (shown here) was on the new line to Pelaw (via Usworth) opened to passengers in 1850 as part of the ECML until superseded by the Team Valley route in 1872. Its importance as a former main line station was still clear in 1958, when it still boasted two booking offices with two different types of pre-grouping NER tickets available at each! On July 19 1958, 'V3' 2—6—2T No. 67691 enters the unusually crowded platform with a special from Usworth to the Durham Miners' Gala. At this time the station had only a spartan regular passenger service (for workers), withdrawn on September 9 1963. *Ian S. Carr.*

Left: Washington station has been utterly erased from the landscape following closure on December 7 1964, as illustrated by this March 15 1987 picture of the diverted 0800 Newcastle-Exeter IC125, passing the station site. *PJR.*

SILKSWORTH COLLIERY is approximately six miles south of Sunderland, and during the 1960s its steeply graded railway became a popular venue for railway photographers who visited to record spectacular efforts by 'J27' 0—6—0s. The Colliery's first rail link was provided in 1871, at its eastern end, to the coastal route and the Londonderry Colliery group maintained this link after the Seaham and Sunderland coastal route was sold to the NER, in 1900. In 1920, when the Lambton & Hetton Colliery Company was in control, a second rail link was constructed, at Silksworth's western end, into the 1822 Hetton Railway. Since 1900, the colliery line had been worked under contract by the NER, and because of steep gradients (averaging 1 in 60) plenty of boiler capacity was required by the locomotives concerned. Class J27 0—6—0s worked the line almost exclusively for the last 30 years or so of steam traction, and pictured here (top) in 1966 is No. 65795, straining at every seam to haul the first evening 'lift' of 'empties' around the Ryhope Colliery yard, and into the last deep cutting before reaching Silksworth. In the distance, a train of 'Vanfits' is running on the coastal route. In 1987 (above) the railway has retreated, leaving the planners to create a landscaped walkway, whilst the terraced houses and allotments on the hillside have given way to modern housing. *Both: PJR.*

SOUTH HETTON COLLIERY: Only an electricity pylon and an electric lamp enable positive identification of this corner of the former railway system at this pit. The first coals to be transported out by rail went down to the boats at Hartlepool via the metals of the Hartlepool Dock and Railway Company running through Wellfield, Castle Eden, Hesledon Dene Bank, Hart and thence the Durham coast through Cemetery North. The 'past' view (above), taken on February 10 1976, shows 'Austerity' 0—6—0ST No. 62, the last operational steam locomotive on the Durham NCB system, taking water, whilst a Hartlepool Class 37 leaves with coal for Teeside. The NCB engineers have gone to some trouble to ensure that locomotive drivers did not have to climb onto the tank-top to take water! *Ray Kitching.*

Above: This view of the same scene in July 1987 illustrates how quickly and completely railway locations can be obliterated. *Ray Kitching.*

ROWLEY, west of Consett, stood in remote hilly country and owed its origins to lead mining and lowland farming. Although the line on which it stands dates from 1834, Rowley station itself did not open until 1846, under the evocative name of Cold Rowley. In 1868 this became plain 'Rowley'. Although not unique, the station building has always been considered unusual with its triple-arched frontage. Rowley also had an island platform as seen in our 1963 photograph (above) as Class K1 2—6—0 No. 62027 passes, in charge of an ambitious five day railtour. In the face of increasing road competition, the handling of lime and ganister (stone) declined, together with passenger traffic, which ended in 1939. The final goods facilities were withdrawn in June 1966, the station being passed thereafter only by Tyne Yard 'trippers' en route to Waskerley, until 1969. The later view (right) shows the abandoned station site in May 1987. *Beamish North of England Open Air Museum/ A.R. Thompson.*

Left: Happily, Rowley station building has been preserved, though not on its original site, for the building has been reconstructed at the North of England Open Air Museum, at Beamish, where it was reopened on August 19 1976 by Sir John Betjeman. The building is now part of an authentic NER tableau, as illustrated in Autumn 1979. *KG.*

KNITSLEY: Knitsley station was situated on the Manchester Valley Branch, approximately two miles east of Consett North Junction. This viaduct could be found a further 1½ miles east of the station, half-way to Manchester village. Work on the branch began in February 1861, using stone brought in from Benton Quarry, (North of Newcastle) for several large bridges were needed, including three structures to span the River Browney, together with two road bridges in Manchester. However, this 700ft long viaduct was constructed mainly in wood, with 36 spans of 20ft each, producing rather a delicate-looking construction of slightly American appearance. It towered 70ft above the Knitsley Burn and its sharp approach curves were a constant worry to the NER. By 1915, the viaduct was in need of major repairs and a decision was taken to turn it into an embankment with the use of colliery slag and spent (used) ballast. This lengthy operation is seen in progress (top) during 1919 — and note the underpass ramparts built in readiness for the 'fill' to be placed around them, at the bottom right. The track was lifted following closure in 1966 and today the embankment survives only as a monument to Victorian and Edwardian railway engineering, as illustrated in the modern view, in 1987. *Beamish North of England Open Air Museum/A.R. Thompson.*

ROWLANDS GILL is in the heart of North Durham, in a vale which became a focal point of the rush by West Durham collieries to transport their coal to the River Tyne for shipment to the south of England for both domestic and industrial use. Rowlands Gill station, on the line between Consett and the Newcastle & Carlisle Railway at Scotswood Bridge, Blaydon, opened on December 2 1867. Coal, brick and timber kept Rowlands Gill goods department busy and classes A8, G5, J39 and laterly K1 locomotives were the staple motive power. Bus competition caused increasing problems for the railway however, and the passenger business ended on September 21 1953; goods traffic continued until November 1965. *W.A. Camwell.*

Top: The neat but deserted station at Rowlands Gill in 1949 as Class V3 2—6—2T No. 7634 (later No. 67634) draws in with a midday Newcastle — Blackhill service. The modern picture (above) reveals that the station has been completely swept away and only a line of platform edging stones, gradually vanishing in the undergrowth, remain as a reminder of this site's railway history. *PJR.*

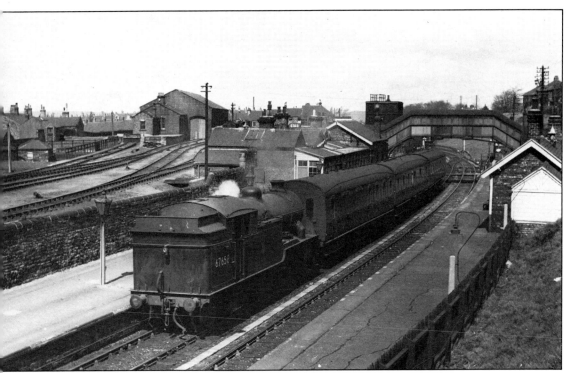

BLACKHILL, on the 'Derwent Valley Line' between Consett and Newcastle started life as Benfieldside on the Blaydon & Consett branch, opened in 1864 and became the focal point for traffic from the Derwent Valley in the north, the early Stanhope & Tyne route from South Shields (via South Pelaw, Annfield and Beamish) the Lanchester branch to Teeside (via the Clarence route) and finally from the south east, via Tow Law. The 'past' view (above) shows Blackhill circa 1950, with Class V1 2—6—2T No. 67658 rolling in with a three-coach train from the Derwent Valley. The last passenger service to serve Blackhill (to Newcastle, via Consett) was withdrawn on May 23 1955, since when the station site has been cleared and landscaped as illustrated in the 'present' view (below) on March 10 1987. *J.F. Sedgwick/PJR.*

MARLEY HILL:, known to railwaymen in the area as Bowes (pronounced Bowser) Bridge is about five miles south-west of Gateshead on the Tanfield Railway, whose lower section was completed as early as 1725. Locomotives were stabled at the line summit from a very early stage, the first official mention being in 1885. Class N10 0—6—2T locomotives were commonly used on this steep line from the early 1900s, and No. 69109, pictured (below) on the turntable in early 1960, was a frequent performer. The building in the background was a modern replacement for the original shed, destroyed by fire in 1942. Steam traction on this route ended in 1962 when the 'N10s' were scrapped and this section closed two years later, though the lower portion from Norwood to Redheugh remained in use into the 1980s for Tyne Yard's Class 03 0—6—0s, to service the Sparton Iron and Steel Works. Today, Bowes Bridge is part of the preserved Tanfield Railway, which runs tourist summer season steam services from Marley Hill to Sunniside. *A.R. Thompson.*

Right: Bowes Bridge on May 25 1987, as Hudswell Clarke 0—4—0ST No. 1672 Irwell (built 1937) passes the over-grown turntable pit with a rake of the TR's home-built four-wheeled passenger carriages bound for Sunniside. *A.R. Thompson.*

FUGAR BAR: Also known as Baker's Bank, this incline was located on the Tanfield Railway, which featured rope haulage and self-acting inclines as well as the use of conventional locomotives, sometimes in rather surprising circumstances. Fugar Bar was on the lower section of the Tanfield line (originating in 1724-5) which was provided to improve on the facilities of the 1699 Dunston wagonway, used to take coal from Blackburn Fell to the staithes at Dunston on Tyne. The 'past' picture, taken in early 1958, shows Class N10 0—6—2Ts Nos. 69097 and 69101 storming the normally rope-worked incline with a maximum load of two hopper wagons of coal destined for household use. The usual method of locomotive working was at the ratio of one wagon per engine from Teams to Sunniside, and the gradients encountered were indeed fierce. The first incline from Lobley Hill Bank, was at an average climb of 1 in 18, whilst the second incline, from Lobley Hill to Sunniside decreased from 1 in 21 to 1 in 33; however, this section also included a short stretch at 1 in 11 (pictured here) easing to 1 in 13, making this the steepest adhesion-worked incline in the country, despite the well-publicised claims about the Hopton Incline, at 1 in 14, in Derbyshire. Fortunately, the gradient board which confirms this fact is displayed at Darlington's North Road Railway Museum. *A.R. Thompson.*

Left: This section of the line closed in 1965 and much of the trackbed is now a public walkway — a policy for which the local authority deserves credit. As illustrated in the modern view, taken in April 1987, the Gateshead — Consett road bridge visible in the old picture has been demolished, the road now crossing the formation at former rail level.
A.R. Thompson.

DURHAM: Perched high above the City centre, adjacent to Wharton Park, Durham station is in a delightful location and commands a magnificent view. Originally a wayside station on the 1856 Leamside — Newton Hall — Bishop Auckland branch, its high construction costs, combined with George Hudson's financial embarrassment crippled the Newcastle & Darlington Railway, which was consequently sold to the York Newcastle & Berwick Railway Company. A unique regular working from the station, mainly on Fridays, were special trains for ailing miners, which worked through to the Conishead Priory convalescent home, near Ulverston. This service, dating from the 1920s, continued until the early 1960s as the last trains to use the trans-Pennine Stainmore route, after mineral traffic ceased in 1960.

The curving southerly approach to the viaduct was always difficult for up through trains, which had to slow to 40mph, though this situation was eased in 1972 when the up platform was set-back to allow a faster approach. Subsequent alterations have included the removal of the up through line. Below: A very unusual visitor to Durham in September 1967 was No. 7029 *Clun Castle,* easing away from the station during cylinder clearance tests prior to the haulage of an enthusiasts special in the north east. Supervising the operation from the cab is John Bellwood, then Newcastle Division Assistant Maintenance Engineer, now Chief Mechanical Engineer for the National Railway Museum, York. Lower: The same spot in 1987; the garden above the station is excellent for train-watching. *Both: KG.*

DURHAM

PLAWSWORTH: North of Durham on the ECML, Plawsworth was a typical rural station in central Durham, equipped with a goods yard, which dealt principally with scrap in the early 1900s. The passenger service ended on April 7 1952, goods facilities being withdrawn in September 1963. The superb 1962 photograph (left) shows an unidentified 'Deltic' (later Class 55) speeding along the down main line towards Tyneside with a Kings Cross — Newcastle express, whilst an 'A4' 4—6—2 relegated to secondary work labours south with a heavy Glasgow — Kings Cross train. The 'A4' was No. 60013 *Dominion of New Zealand*, built in 1937 at Doncaster and which spent most of its working life based at 'Top Shed' (King's Cross). It was recognisable by its large deep-pitched whistle, fitted in May 1939 as a gift from the New Zealand Government and bought by the Festiniog Railway when the engine was withdrawn in April 1963. Incidentally, this whistle was later stolen and has never been returned to its owners. *A.R. Thompson.*

Right: Plawsworth much overgrown, on July 3 1987; No. 47406 *Railriders* is at the head of the 1425 Newcastle — Liverpool Trans-pennine service. There is no trace today of the small country station and its signalbox and goods yard. *PJR.*

DEERNESS VALLEY JUNCTION: This complex of lines near Relly Mill, south of Durham, was both impressive and important, and had a station been built here, it would undoubtedly have been the North East's answer to Crewe! The first railway on the scene here was the Durham — Bishop Auckland line of 1856, followed in 1858 by a westwards route to Ushaw Moor. In 1862, the route from Consett, along the Lanchester Valley, came in from the left (west) and in 1872 the current ECML came into being. The final development, as shown in the oldest picture (opposite page, upper) was the construction of an underpass beneath the Bishop Auckland line, linking the Consett route with the ECML at Bridge House Junction, and also a link from the Consett line to the Deerness Valley route. The oldest view (opposite page, upper) shows English Electric Type 4 (later Class 40) No. D240 heading for Bishop Auckland on July 17 1960, with a diverted Newcastle — King's Cross express. In the background is the tightly curved (and speed restricted) ECML and D240 is about to cross the Consett — Bridge House underpass. On the left, 'Q6' 0—8—0 No. 63448 waits to follow the express onto the Bishop Auckland route with finished steel products from

Consett. Delays were common at this water column, and on a previous occasion an enterprising footplate artist had painted three figures on the wall of the adjacent permanent way cabin. They represent an engine driver ('Faith'), a fireman ('Hope') and a guard ('Charity') and this artistic work survived for many years, as illustrated in the circa 1967 view (opposite page, lower) by which time the Consett links had been lifted. Following the closure of the Bishop Auckland line to passenger traffic in May 1964, and subsequently to all traffic on August 5 1968, the way was clear for realignment of the ECML, whose tight curvature was eased considerably to enable a higher line speed at this point. Thus, the course taken by No. 45137 *The Bedfordshire and Hertfordshire Regiment (TA)*, in charge of the 1605 Newcastle — Liverpool of June 15 1986, utilises the area formerly occupied by the Bishop Auckland line and the Consett underpass. The complex junction is now a simple main line layout and 'Faith, Hope and Charity' have passed into the annals of railway lore.

Ian S. Carr/Beamish North of England Open Air Museum/PJR.

DEERNESS VALLEY JUNCTION: This shows the view looking south at Relly Mill, south of Durham (compare with northerly view, pages 74 & 75). English Electric Type 4 (later Class 40) No. D259 (top) carrying the white indicator discs of an express freight duty, is leading a down freight off the Bishop Auckland line on June 19 1960, with the Waterhouses branch diverging to the right. In the distance is Brandon Colliery. Deerness Valley Junction signalbox had a commanding view of the routes under its control, but it closed on December 28 1964 and the impressive junction was subsequently swept away. The 'present' view (above) shows the desolate scene in March 1987. The ECML passes to the left of this field of view. *Robert Leslie/PJR.*

CROXDALE: The attractive little station at Croxdale is another railway facility which has been utterly erased from the landscape. Located between Ferryhill and Durham, passenger traffic was always sparse and the station closed on September 26 1938. The past picture (above) taken circa 1910, is a railway modellers delight — note the marvellous cantilevered bracket signal, the gas lamps and the brick and wooden platform buildings. The picture has an unhurried air of the Sunday morning nonchalance of the Edwardian era. *Beamish North of England Open Air Museum.*

Above: On July 9 1987, a Class 47 diesel electric locomotive passes the site of Croxdale station with empty pipe-carrying wagons from St. Neots, bound for Leith. The basic bridge structure remains unchanged, although now surmounted by a brick wall, rather than the distinctive station building shown in the old picture. *PJR.*

PITTINGTON was approximately three miles north-east of Durham and the 'past' picture shows Class G5 0—4—4T No. 67251 standing at the platform in 1948. Pittington at this time was the terminus of the old Durham & Sunderland route which originally ran into Durham Elvet. The Pittington line was operating by 1837, through Sherburn (on the outskirts of Durham), but the aim of reaching the city centre was never achieved. Pittington retained its passenger service until January 1953, when Ryhope, Murton and Hetton stations also closed. The 'G5s' were fitted with push-and-pull equipment by the 1940s, eliminating the need for the engine to run round its train before returning to Sunderland. The modern picture (below) shows the station site in April 1987, when just a remnant of platform remained in situ. *W.A. Camwell/PJR.*

MID-DURHAM COUNTY

SHILDON STATION SOUTH JUNCTION: On February 10 1983 (top) Class 31 No. 31290 draws its train of wagonsprings, wheels and axleboxes off the Shildon works branch, past Shildon Signal Box, (near the site of the original Stockton & Darlington Railway main line) towards Darlington, via the site of Thickley Sidings (once claimed as the largest in the world) and Heighington. Note the remains of the Stockton & Darlington coaldrops (in the 'Y' of the junction) near the foot of the Black Boy Incline (1828). The drops served as a coaling stage for Shildon locomotive shed until about 1935. Derelict to the left of the drops is the private Soho Works of Timothy Hackworth, the house of which is now a railway museum dedicated to his memory. The signal box shown here, first known as Shildon Junction, became Shildon South in 1936 and then plain 'Shildon' in 1967, following the closure of Shildon North signalbox. *David Allen.*

Above: The same scene today is much changed, following closure of Shildon Works in 1984. The works branch survives only as a truncated 'neck', the SDR coaldrops now bordering an abandoned wasteland which was once a hive of railway activity. On June 2 1987, the 1333 DMU from Bishop Auckland passes the photographer, bound for Saltburn. *A.R. Thompson.*

SHILDON WORKS: The loss of Shildon Works was an especially bitter and sad blow to the railway community in the north east, especially considering the town's past contributions and skills. The Works was constructed in 1833 on the site of Timothy Hackworth's plant of the early 1820s, giving the site an indisputable claim to be the cradle of large-scale locomotive building. In latter days, the Works concentrated on wagon building and the 18-month struggle to save the Works is now history, but it was a 'bonnie fight', as local people might describe it, and it is interesting to look back over the newspaper reports and summarise the sequence of events:

February 2 1983:	BR Workers faced forced redundancy with the proposed Shildon closure.		jects unions pleas for works retention, but meets NUR officials at Shildon.
February 19 1983:	BR responds that BREL plans to close Shildon and Horwich may be revised.	July 31 1983:	Corporate plan leak; 20,000 more BR jobs to be lost nationwide.
March 3 1983:	Michael Foot pledges to save the Works in his 'Shildon speech'.	August 2 1983:	Shildon Works closure notices are rejected by all workers.
April 10 1983:	BR announces that 4,500 jobs will be lost at Shildon.	August 5 1983:	BR workers reject strike plan regarding Shildon Works closure.
May 10 1983:	Union strike is threatened over Shildon closure.	October 12 1983:	NUR proposes a reprieve for Shildon; rejected by BR.
July 22 1983:	BR turns down workshop plans proposed by unions.	June 20 1984:	Gates close after last shift, at 1500.
July 29 1983:	Transport Minister Tom King re-	March 1985:	Works branch track removal begins.
		May 1985:	Track removal complete.

Our 'past' picture (opposite page, top) illustrates one of Shildon's last great moments, as host to the locomotives present for the 1975 celebrations to mark the 150th anniversary of the opening of the Stockton & Darlington Railway. The present view from the same spot shows the works site in the cold light of a wintry day on March 7 1987 (opposite page, lower) with all track removed and buildings sold-off piecemeal to light industrial users. A reminder of the past exists in the new name given to the complex — the Hackworth Industrial Park. The third picture of the works (above) shows an interior scene in Edwardian days, with mineral hoppers under repair. *John Hunt/PJR/National Railway Museum.*

FERRYHILL: This was an extensive and important railway junction, where routes from all four points of the compass converged to produce a centre of great interest. Below: A general view of Ferryhill, looking south towards Darlington, on September 2 1968, by which time a general air of decline was clearly apparent, although the layout was still impressive. In the background is Mainsforth Colliery, whilst the yard in the foreground houses a coal depot of a type once very common, but which are now increasingly scarce. The station's overgrown north-facing bay once served Spennymoor branch services — and note the NER water column at the platform end. Beyond the station are extensive areas of standage for loaded mineral and limestone trains. *Ray Goad.*

Right: Following the progressive loss of its various local passenger services to Bishop Auckland, Stockton, Spennymoor, West Hartlepool Castle Eden, Wellfield, Sunderland, Leamside, Penshaw and Pelaw, the main line station at Ferryhill closed on March 6 1967. This view depicts Class 45 No. 45137 *The Bedfordshire & Hertfordshire Regiment (TA)* passing the much simplified station site with the 0620 Liverpool — Newcastle service of May 30 1987. The goods yard is long gone and the colliery has been cleared and landscaped, whilst a limestone terminal now occupies the site of the former holding sidings beyond the enlarged road bridge. *PJR.*

SPENNYMOOR: Situated on the Clarence Railway branch from Ferryhill to Byers Manor, Spennymoor station featured a bi-directional single platform. This was a mineral area, so passenger traffic was always sparse and the regular service from Ferryhill was withdrawn on March 31 1952. Holiday 'specials' still ran occasionally however, and our 'past' picture (above) shows Spennymoor on June 2 1963, as Riddles '4MT' No. 76050 rolls in with IZ05, a Whit Sunday excursion from Bishop Auckland to Seaton Carew. No. 76050 was withdrawn from service in September 1966 and was scrapped within two months by Shipbreaking Industries of Faslane. *F.R. Tweddle.*

Above: This was one of the most difficult locations to precisely identify today, and was only achieved after much map study and 'stalking' of the town itself! Very few common features remain, such as the buildings on the extreme left, immediately above the 'keep left' bollard! Today, Bank Holiday excursions from Spennymoor are doubtless taken by car, with much time being spent in endless 'traffic jams'. *A.R. Thompson.*

BRANCEPETH: Located between Bishop Auckland and Deerness Valley Junction (see pages 75 and 76), Brancepeth lay adjacent to the castle and park grounds of the same name. Passenger traffic survived until May 4 1964, goods facilities being withdrawn three months later. Our 'past' photograph (top) taken on September 19 1965, is unusual, for 'A4s' were far from common on these metals; No. 60004 *William Whitelaw* was working the highly successful RCTS 'Blyth and Tyne' railtour, from Leeds. *PJR.*

Above: Brancepeth, pictured in 1987, long after the railway had departed, and with the formation now in use only by wildlife and the occasional hiker. This area was once a hive of mining activity, but with the closure over the years of pits at Brandon, Browney, Oakenshaw, Bowden Close and Brancepeth itself, the once familiar pithead winding gear has passed into the history books. *PJR.*

BISHOP AUCKLAND: This was an interesting triangular station of which only a small part survives today. Links to Durham, Ferryhill and Barnard Castle have all gone, leaving the town served nowadays only by the old SDR route. On May 22 1965 (below) Gresley 'V2' 2—6—2 No. 60884 is ready to leave Platform 3 at Bishop Auckland with a Territorial Army special working to Cheltenham. The train is standing on the Durham route, which closed to passengers on May 4 1964. *Ray Goad.*

Left: The June 1987 view at this location presents a very different scene, a station car park having replaced curving platforms 2 and 3 and their graceful cast iron and glass curving canopies. BR's provincial DMU services still serve Bishop Auckland, though from a much shortened platform. This is the deepest incursion into West Durham made by BR's passenger services (from Saltburn) in the late 1980s for although the route beyond to Eastgate survives today it is used by freight services to the Blue Circle cement works. This region gave railways to the world, and it is very sad indeed to see its own routes in such sad decline. *PJR.*

TOW LAW, in West Durham, occupied a strategic point between the east coast ports and the rich mineral tracts in the hills to the west. The first railway to come to Tow Law was the SDR, via Shildon and Bishop Auckland. The surrounding terrain was difficult, but eventually, via the Sunniside incline, the SDR was able to connect with the Stanhope & Tyne Railway. This subsequently became a through Darlington — Newcastle route, as an alternative to the Lanchester branch, having the common point of Blackhill station, prior to the Derwent Valley descent to Scotswood. The old picture (below) shows Tow Law in 1954, as Class A5/2 4—6—2T No 69883 pauses with a Darlington-bound train. Closed in 1965, the station has since been completely erased and the precise location of the scene for the modern photograph (lower) was difficult: the only common building is the house visible in the 'past' picture between the signalbox and the train. It can still be seen (albeit extended) in the centre background of the later view on July 14 1987. *J. House/PJR.*

WEST DURHAM

ST. JOHN'S CHAPEL: In May 1962, Class J26 0—6—0 No. 65735 passes time at St. John's Chapel whilst working the thrice-weekly pick-up goods from Bishop Auckland. This branch developed very much in 'fits and starts' and it was not until 1895 that rails penetrated the mineral country West of Stanhope, through Johns Chapel, to Wearhead. It had taken 52 years and five distinct phases of construction to reach this far west! The passenger service became extinct on June 29 1953 and St. John's Chapel station has since been completely obliterated, its site is today occupied by a modern industrial unit. A small outbuilding in the centre distance links the two scenes. *Both: Ian S. Carr.*

WINSTON: Located mid-way between Darlington and Barnard Castle, Winston opened in July 1856. From the outset, traffic was never heavy, but trains occasionally required strengthening on market days. Our oldest picture (above) shows the attractive station (looking east) in 1895, the station nameboard proclaiming 'Winston for Staindrop'. The goods warehouse wall carries an impressive array of enamel advertisements. Goods services were withdrawn from Winston on April 5 1964, passenger services surviving until November that year. *N. Mackay Collection.*

Left: The remains of Winston station on June 16 1987. The modified station buildings are still in use and the platform remnant betrays the railway past. The goods shed survives, though its enamel adverts are long gone and a vehicle inspection ramp occupies part of the former trackbed. *Ray Goad.*

BARNARD CASTLE: We were fortunate to locate two historic pictures taken from the same spot at Barnard Castle station, enabling us to provide a fascinating triple view spanning 51 years. Sited on the West Durham/Yorkshire county boundary, Barnard Castle had a collective village population of more than 7,000 people by 1911, in which year 66,714 passengers booked tickets at the station. Running through wild countryside, the line was not easy to build and always expensive to maintain. The Penrith-Barnard Castle passenger service was withdrawn on January 22 1962, and the Barnard Castle-Bishop Auckland service closed in June 1962. Finally, the Barnard Castle-Darlington service closed on November 30 1964.

Top: Barnard Castle circa 1935, showing GNR 4—4—0 No. 4354, an elderly locomotive which had probably been displaced from its former express duties by more modern classes. Barnard Castle had its own engine shed at this time, but it closed in 1937. *Beamish North of England Open Air Museum.*

Above: The same location on July 24 1957, as 'G5' No. 67258 runs round its train before returning to Sunderland, via Penshaw. The track layout and signalbox appear unchanged, but a neat row of bushes has appeared between the tracks and the NER lower quadrant semaphores have been replaced by more modern upper quadrant signals. *Ian S. Carr.*

Right: Following closure, Barnard Castle station was completely obliterated and today, only the trees on the right help positively identify the location of the once neat platforms. The station site is now occupied by a Glaxo works and car park. *Ian S. Carr.*

MIDDLETON IN TEESDALE: Although technically in Yorkshire, this station's trains served County Durham and is therefore featured in these pages in the aim for logical coverage. In the old picture (top) Class G5 0—4—4T No. 67258 stands against the stopblock at Middleton-in-Teesdale after working the 8.23am train from Sunderland which this locomotive worked from Durham, on July 24 1957. Opened in May 1868 and closed on November 30 1964, the station (renowned for its station gardens) was nine miles north west of Barnard Castle and ½-mile from the village it served. The small one-engine shed closed in 1957 and DMUs started plying the branch — though they were usually almost empty. Freight services were withdrawn in 1965 and in many ways it was surprising that passenger traffic survived until as late as 1964. Caravans occupy the station site today.
Both: Ian S. Carr.

STAINMORE: This name will forever be associated with steam locomotives struggling over difficult gradients, in wild weather. Stainmore was the summit of the trans-Pennine mineral route which ran west from Barnard Castle over Bowes Moor and into Cumbria, to eventually run through Kirkby Stephen to connect with West Coast Main Line. The line closed to passengers on January 22 1962, almost 100 years to the day after its completion.

Top: In 1952, Ivatt '4MT' 2—6—0 No. 43018 passes Stainmore with a mixed goods, assisted by a banking engine. Following closure and demolition, this section of trackbed was used to enable the A66 to be converted into a dual carriageway, as illustrated in our July 1987 view (above). How many of the drivers passing this point realise that they are running over the site of a former railway where footplatemen worked very much against the odds to keep their trains rolling? As illustrated in *No. 1* of this *Past & Present* series, covering Cumbria, the NER trackbed of this route between Ravenstonedale and Tebay has also been used to ease the route of the A66 trunk road. *Cecil Ord/PJR.*

DARLINGTON

DARLINGTON WORK: Before the railway arrived, Darlington was a simple Saxon town on the River Skerne, notorious for its hard working Quaker families who had settled in 1660 and established a strong textile trade. However, the rural district was transformed utterly in 1825 by the opening of the SDR and the town became the focal point of industrial revolution. The SDR's main locomotive works, at Shildon, turned increasingly to wagon construction when Darlington North Road Locomotive Works opened in 1863. Darlington became the NER's chief works, and activity was intense throughout the LNER period and even into early BR days. Darlington built examples of Robert Riddles Standard range of steam locomotives, and new construction continued until 1964, when the last new diesel, No. D7597, rolled out of the erecting shop. Locomotive overhauls continued until closure on April 2 1966. The once-busy workshops were demolished. Our 'past' view shows the erecting shop on October 30 1965, locomotives undergoing overhaul including 'J27' 0—6—0 No. 65880, 'K1' 2—6—0 No. 62004 and 'WD' 2—8—0 No. 90503. The later view shows the sad appearance of this location in March 1987. *Both: PJR.*

DARLINGTON WORKS SCRAP YARD: The cutting up of condemned locomotives at Darlington Works was an extremely public operation, as this sad activity was easily viewed from North Road station, visible in the background of the modern picture (right, upper) taken in February 1987, BR's provincial services to Bishop Auckland still use North Road, which also houses the town's railway museum. The old picture at this location (right, lower) depicts the sad demolition of LNER Class D20 4—4—0s No. 62375 and 62383. Work is slightly more advanced on No. 62375, the splasher having been removed and a start made on the removal of pipework and plating. Chalked on the smokebox door is the word 'Farewell' and lying in the 'four foot' in front of No. 62375 are a selection of plain axles and the remains of a crank axle. What a waste of precision engineering! The rear three-quarter view of No. 62383 emphasises the large 6ft 10in diameter driving wheels and rear splasher. Introduced in 1899 by Wilson Worsdell, the 'D20' 4—4—0s performed stalwart service, latterly on secondary duties in the border regions, until they disappeared from service in May 1957. How many locomotives were destroyed on this small patch of land, now occupied by a small park? *Both: PJR.*

STOCKTON & DARLINGTON CROSSING: Darlington's famous flat crossing, situated near Parkgate, exists now in memory only, and whilst trains still pass the site, you have to be very sharp to identify the location today as you race past on the ECML. The west-east route was the first railway on this site, as part of the SDR's main line between North Road station and Fighting Cocks, but fame came when the Newcastle and Darlington main line was extended north, thereby producing the flat crossing. The crossing was completed in 1844 and the 'inevitable' occurred on December 8 1860 when an up NER goods sliced through the centre portion of an SDR mineral train, the driver of which had become 'lost' in thick fog. Following the opening of the new Darlington Bank Top station, this route lost its passenger service in 1887. The old picture (top) shows a diverted Darlington-Saltburn service, running via the original route, behind Class A8 4—6—2T No. 69892. The SDR route was singled in May 1956 and subsequently closed on May 21 1967, with the completion of the Darlington resignalling scheme. The later picture shows the former crossing site on February 21 1987 as an IC 125 sprints north. *J.W. Armstrong/KG.*

BARTON GOODS: This goods station was actually in Yorkshire, though its railway originated west of Darlington, on the Barnard Castle route. This curious goods line, which always struggled for its traffic, is little-known, and photographs are rare. The line was authorised by Act of Parliament in 1866 and completed four years later; it eventually became part of the NER in 1890. Traffic was always sparse, primarily from Melsonby Quarries, and after this ended in the early 1950s, Barton Goods lay derelict until 1963 (as shown above), when surveyors began looking for an appropriate route for the new A1(M) road planned for just north of Scotch Corner — the much-needed Darlington area by-pass. This north-easterly railway route was judged to be ideal and in early 1964 work began. The railway cutting, an average of 12ft wide at rail level, was opened out to the minimum motorway width of 102 feet, with an overall upper width of 200 feet. The finished road provides a graphic illustration of how much more space a road occupies in the landscape compared with a railway. The modern picture was taken on June 21 1987. The hut on the right provides a solitary element of continuity. *K.L. Taylor Collection/R. Goad*

Stockton & Teeside

STOCKTON: The first public railway in the world to be operated by steam traction opened in September 1825 between Stockton Cottage Row, Darlington and Etherley. The NER subsequently decided to build a new larger station further east, and the changing appearance of this station is depicted on this page. Top: A bustling scene at the north end of Stockton station, during the 1950s, as 'K3' 2—6—0 No. 61875 takes water before departing with a down express passenger service. The impressive station roof was 80ft wide and almost 560ft long — a worthy station for one of the towns which gave public railways to the world. Stockton's fortunes as an important railway centre have faded considerably in the last three decades, as illustrated by the modern view (above) on March 7 1987, after the loss of the roof. The track layout has been severely curtailed and the busy bay platform roads have been stripped away and replaced by a row of saplings. K. Linford/PJR.

STOCKTON MPD: This 1959 view (right, upper) shows the Stockton 'new shed' of 1894, which was equipped with eight roads. The shed provided traction mainly for local work, with crews generally travelling no further than either Leeds or Sunderland. The majority of duties encompassed Wellfield, Ferryhill, Hartlepool and occasionally south of the Tees, towards Redcar and Battersby Junction on the Whitby route. The closure of Stockton freight sidings in 1930 limited locomotive requirements but this yard was rejuvenated during the Second World War, when Stockton's allocation increased to more than 50 locomotives. In 1959, locomotives on shed included 'J26' 0—6—0s, 'K1' 2—6—0 No. 62001, 'B1' 4—6—0 No. 61220, 'J94' 0—6—0ST No. 68049 and 'K1' No. 62042. The shed closed during 1959, its 31 engines being dispersed to other depots. *Bill Hampson.*

Right, lower: Stockton shed in March 1987, in use as a factory — but note that an extension has been built on the right. *PJR.*

HAVERTON HILL: On the north bank of the Tees, some six miles from the estuary, lies Haverton Hill, midway between Port Clarence and Billingham. Passenger services were an early casualty on this route and the station closed on March 1 1954, leaving only a workmens service, which lingered until November 6 1961. Our 1950s picture (below, right) shows an afternoon workers train waiting to leave for Billingham in the charge of 'A5/2' 4—6—2T No. 69842. The station, which spanned a busy road, had an unusually 'temporary' air, with fencing built onto the roof slopes of adjacent houses, accompanied by scout-hut-style waiting rooms. Note the vintage NER semaphore, used to control reversals into a siding.

Below, left: Haverton Hill on July 15 1987, with some background chimney stacks remaining to identify the location — albeit with fewer pots. Only a single track remains today, and co-author Ken Groundwater occupies the former up main line! *Michael Rhodes.*

BILLINGHAM ON TEES: These pictures show the site west of Billingham 'old' station, where goods loops provided additional run-around and stabling space for trains awaiting main line paths. The old view (above) on October 20 1966 shows Class K1 2—6—0 No. 62041 standing on the down goods loop, on the old Leeds Northern main line route from Northallerton to Stockton, with a train of Dolomite from Thrislington (Ferryhill), for the Steetly magnesite works, at Cemetery North. Behind the 'K1' are standing another two goods trains; a 'WD' 2—8—0 with coal 'empties' from Haverton Hill to Murton and a Class 24 diesel with a short pick-up 'tripper' from Tees Yard. In the foreground, Class Q6 0—8—0 No. 63394 is running round its train to reverse direction, having arrived with coal from South Hetton, bound for the ICI complex at Haverton Hill. The loops were substantial: the down side being 1,447 yards in length and the up loop 1,341 yards long. *J.M. Boyes.*

Left: In common with many other locations, rationalisation has left only a plain double track section at Billingham, as pictured on July 15 1987 as Class 143 railbus scurries past the sole surviving semaphore arm on the bracketed post on the right. *KG.*

BILLINGHAM ON TEES: These pictures present an interesting contrast of the changing face of north eastern coal traffic by rail. Top: On November 4 1966, 'Q6' 0—8—0 No. 63426, which is far from steam tight at the front end, is labouring through Billingham 'old' station with a West Hartlepool — Haverton Hill coal train. Note the loading gauge on the left. The station in the background closed on November 7 1966, just three days after this picture was taken. The modern view of the same location reveals many changes: the station buildings and platforms have been swept away, and replaced by a new station ½-mile to the east, whilst the goods yard, closed in November 1978, has been redeveloped with private houses. The signalbox remains to oversee the busy level crossing, and whilst a couple of semaphore signals survived on July 15 1987, the sidings have all been stripped away to leave a plain double track section. No. 56128 is approaching with a MGR coal train from Easington to York. *J.M. Boyes/KG.*

RAILWAYS AROUND
HARTLEPOOL

HARTLEPOOL NEWBURN: On June 8 1967 (above) the 1200 Newcastle — York parcels (coastal) service passes Newburn behind 'Peak' (now Class 45) No. D 182, on the alignment of the original West Hartlepool Harbour & Railway Company, which amalgamated with the NER in 1865. The scene is rich in railway atmosphere with an extensive track layout, semaphore signals, lineside point rodding and signal wires, historic stock and interesting buildings, including the locomotive sheds on the left and the wagon repair shops in the centre background. Newburn signalbox dated from 1912. Occasionally, a 'breaker' would clear the wall at this location, sometimes soaking an unsuspecting steam locomotive crew on an old open-cab locomotive! *John M. Boyes.*

Right: The bleak view greeting the photographer from the same spot on July 15 1987, as a DMU rumbled past, heading for Middlesbrough. The true meaning of the term rationalisation is painfully apparent, the signalbox, shed, and much of the layout having passed into history. Only the two main lines and an up loop remain. *KG.*

WELLFIELD: This was once an important East Durham railway 'crossroads', where the north-south line between Sunderland and Teeside crossed the east-west route from Hart to Ferryhill. Both routes have since disappeared from the railway map. Wellfield station, just behind the photographer, was opened in 1882 to provide connections between the Hartlepool, Sunderland and Stockton services. The passenger service south of Wellfield closed late in 1931, but the public service on the Sunderland — West Hartlepool line continued until June 9 1952. The opening of the coastal route, via Seaham, dealt a fatal blow to the passenger potential of the Wellfield route, which remained in use for chiefly mineral traffic, as illustrated (right, upper) as 'Q6' 0—8—0 No. 63387 storms past with coal hoppers, in August 1967. On March 7 1987 (right, lower) the abandoned route was in use only as a footpath by a solitary winter walker. *Both: PJR.*

SHOTTON COLLIERY EXCHANGE SIDINGS: Shotton, in the heartland of Central East Durham mining country, was utterly dependent on coal. The Great Northern coalfield had since 1822 been exploited in coastal Durham and the new pits were large and deep, burrowing through magnesian limestone to the rich seams beneath. The coalfields flourished because they were near the sea, and the railways worked hard to transport the coal to the quaysides, where hundreds of collier brigs crowded the seaward horizon. Sunderland South Dock, Seaham and Hartlepool were the principal outlets, linked by many railways to the numerous pits.

Statistics compiled by D.J. Rowe based on the 1861 census show that 18.2% of Durham's working population were engaged in the coal industry, while only 7% were working in agriculture. The older view (top) depicts Shotton Colliery exchange sidings circa 1967, with a Barclay 0—4—0ST and a Class 37 diesel going about their business with the hopper wagons. Since closure, the Shotton Colliery Industrial Estate and green area have replaced the mining complex, and the characteristic pithead gear and grimy sidings have disappeared, as illustrated (above). *Malcolm Dunnett/ Ray Kitching.*

SEAHAM: Seaham Harbour evolved principally because of the endeavours of Lord Londonderry (Earl Vane), whose plans to make this a huge shipping centre were only impeded by the daunting cliffs bordering his Seaham estate, acquired in 1828. By 1840 it became clear that the existing facilities were both inadequate and incapable of economic extension. A temporary arrangement implemented in 1852 was — the diversion of traffic via Rainton and the Durham — Sunderland line, via Seaton Bank top. A more permanent solution was the construction of a coastal route to Sunderland, opened on August 3 1854 and which by 1906 was the main NER route to Hartlepool. Our 'past' picture (above) shows Seaham Docks, circa 1870 — note that the ships are all still sailing vessels. On October 7 1900, the NER took over the docks ending 46 years of rule by a sole private proprietor. *Beamish North of England Open Air Museum.*

Right: Seaham Harbour in 1987, with many of the original quays still intact, despite modernisation. Under the ownership of the Seaham Harbour Dock company, a promising future appears likely, and as a reminder of times past a single chauldron (above) stands guard at the main gate. *Both: KG.*

HART, some three miles north of Hartlepool, was at the convergence of the NER's extension of the coastal route (on the right) with the Ryhope — Seaton — Wellfield — Castle Eden line (on the left). Class A1 4—6—2 No. 60154 *Bon Accord* is pictured racing away from Hesledon Bank with a weekend diversion from the coastal route, during March 1954. The Wellfield route lost its passenger service in June 1952, freight services continuing into the late 1960s. Hart station closed on August 31 1953, and as shown on March 7 1987 (below) the coastal route now sweeps past the site of the wooden platforms and the abandoned trackbed. The DMU was working a Newcastle — Middlesbrough service. *Bob Payne/PJR.*

ACKNOWLEDGEMENTS

IN addition to those photographic contributors credited throughout this book, special thanks are due to Ian S. Carr, Bill Hampson and particularly Alan Thompson, who not only helped out with printing when PJR's enlarger expired under the workload, but also foolishly volunteered to find the present location of the Spennymoor picture!

Ray Goad and many other North Eastern Railway Association members also gave much valued assistance and checked captions, for which we were very grateful. Their unique knowledge of all things 'North Eastern' was a great asset. Professor Norman McCord of the University of Newcastle's History Department opened his extensive files in typical selfless attitude and gave some useful leads, for which we would like to record our thanks.

Robin Gard, his staff and members of the Association of Northumberland Local History Societies were patient with our constant 'badgering' for records office (Gosforth) material,

and our thanks are sincerely given. Thanks also to Michael Halbert, Bob Payne and Dave Tyreman, for searching their collections for suitable material, and also to another (former) railwayman, Ken Appleby, who helped add interesting details to many captions.

British Rail Area Management also helped by granting permission to visit their property to take photographs on those few occasions it became absolutely necessary; this assistance was much appreciated.

Few of the people we approached were reluctant to lend material and the one regret we have is that a planned meeting with Jack Armstrong, an excellent NER photographer, didn't materialise due to his sad and sudden death. A few of his photographs have been used, with permission of his family, as a tribute to his interest in the earlier stages of the preparation of this book, and his creditable efforts to record a passing moment in the railway history of the north east.

REAR COVER: SILVER LINK AT NEWCASTLE CENTRAL STATION: The appearance of pioneer streamlined 'A4' 4—6—2 No. 2509 *Silver Link* in September 1935 sent a shock wave through the railway world, for although streamlining had already been experimented with in France, as early as 1894, its arrival in Britain provoked strong reactions. *Silver Link* was actually the first of four such 'streamliners' with which LNER Chief Mechanical Engineer H.N. Gresley aimed to completely transform the East Coast Main Line — thereby sowing the seeds of our own current High Speed Train service. *Silver Link's* first test run for engineers and press representatives was a startling success, for on September 27 1935, the 'A4' was unleashed on a trip from King's Cross to Grantham and reached a top speed of 112.5mph, a new British speed record. The locomotive was an immediate technical and commercial success, and the travelling public seized the chance to ride aboard the 'Silver Jubilee' with its beautiful silver painted coaches.

The next development for the streamlined 'A4s' was the inauguration of the 'Coronation' express, on July 5 1937. This streamlined service featured only one stop between Edinburgh and London, at Newcastle, and the journey time was six hours between the Capitals. This 1938 picture of the 'Coronation' at Newcastle features No. 2509 in silver-grey livery, prior to the LNER's adoption of garter blue as the standard livery for the class. The HST seen in the modern photograph, taken on May 31 1987, bears striking similarities, not only in general shape but also with its fixed train formations. The HST is pictured in precisely the same location as No. 2509, though the station roof has since been cut-back. THe HSTs are also a success story in the true tradition of the East Coast Main Line, and their utilisation is relentlessly intense, as illustrated by this typical day in the life of one set. An HST leaves London Kings Cross at 0630 and after a 1,050-miles return trip to Aberdeen will return to Kings Cross just before midnight, after which it runs empty to Bounds Green depot for fuelling, cleaning and servicing, before beginning another cyclic diagram of equal mileage the following morning. The fixed formations have ended the operators 'on the spot' flexibility to strengthen busy trains as necessary, but this is a small price to pay against excellent value for money — although passengers on tightly packed peak-hour HST's may not agree! *W.B. Greenfield (Courtesy NELPG)/PJR.*